W9-AJO-837

The
Federalist
Papers
Reader

and
Historical
Documents
of Our
American Heritage

The
Federalist
Papers
Reader

and

Historical

Documents

of Our

American Heritage

Frederick Quinn, Editor

Preface by Warren E. Burger
Foreword by A.E. Dick Howard

SEVEN LOCKS PRESS

Santa Ana, California
Minneapolis, Minnesota
Washington, D.C.

Library of Congress Cataloging-in-Publication Data

The Federalist Papers Reader and Historical Documents of our American Heritage /
    Frederick Quinn, editor ; preface by Warren E. Burger ; foreword by
    A.E. Dick Howard.
            p. cm.
    Includes bibliographical references and index.
    ISBN 0-929765-58-3
    1. Consitutional history--United States--Sources. 2. United States--Politics and
    government--Sources. I. Quinn, Frederick.
KF4515.F43   1997
320.973'09'033--dc21

                                                    97-28854
                                                    CIP

Manufactured in the United States of America

Seven Locks Press
PO Box 25689
Santa Ana, CA 92799
(800) 354-5348

To Alison and Christopher

Table of Contents

Foreword

Democratization is in the air all over the world; from Albania and Brazil to Bulgaria and South Africa, fundamental questions about how to govern human society are being debated in parliament and press, among trade unionists and university students, entrepreneurs and constitutionalists.

The questions asked and the language of political discourse bear amazing similarities to those debated in America in 1787, when thirteen unruly, independent states took the radical step of uniting under an untried Constitution. Issues of separation of powers, checks and balances, the independence of the judiciary, and federalism were central to making this relatively short document both work in its immediate context and survive for over two centuries.

The Federalist Papers are both an explanation of why the Constitution emerged the way it did and, no less important, how the Founders understood human political behavior. Frederick Quinn has chosen carefully from among the original eighty-five essays, selecting twenty-three that reflect enduring wisdom about constitution writing in the contemporary world. His introductory essay, with admirable economy, frames the issues and describes the personalities, and his comments on key essays will be of value to students of the U.S. Constitution and the constitutional process in the United States or abroad.

Frederick Quinn brings unique skills to this task. As International Coordinator for the Bicentennial of the U.S. Constitution, he worked closely with former Chief Justice of the United States Warren E. Burger in advancing a global scholarly exchange among constitutionalists. As a foreign service officer and historian, he experienced firsthand the debate on basic issues of governance in embassies in Morocco, Burkina Faso, Haiti, Vietnam, Cameroon, and Czechoslovakia in times of political upheaval.

In particular, in Czechoslovakia, where he worked closely with the Charter '77 dissident community, questions of rule "by the one, the many, or the few" were active issues over which citizens died, were imprisoned, suffered deprivation of rights and property, and emerged ultimately with individual freedom and collective independence.

The Federalist Papers Reader is a timely and valuable guide for the modern reader on how James Madison, Alexander Hamilton, and John Jay interpreted the most basic issues of human politics and how, faced with perilous choices, they and the Founders established a Constitution that endures. They shaped a society that prospers, despite its imperfections, and a legal system that, flaws notwithstanding, contains the tumult of clashing factions that Madison witnessed and that have destroyed ordered government in countless states in recent history.

— **A.E. Dick Howard**
White Burkett Miller Professor
of Law and Public Affairs
University of Virginia Law School

Preface

Near the close of the Constitutional Convention of 1787, Benjamin Franklin, the elder statesman of the convention, commented to those sitting near him "that painters had found it difficult to distinguish in their art a rising sun from a setting sun." Then, while looking at the rising sun carved on the back of George Washington's chair, he stated, "I have . . . often and in the course of the session . . . looked at that behind the president without being able to tell whether it was rising or setting. But now at length I have the happiness to know that it is a rising sun and not a setting sun."

Benjamin Franklin's statement proved to be prophetic—in more ways than one. Two hundred years after the fact, it is tempting to look upon the convention and the events that followed and focus strictly on the remarkable document the delegates created—our Constitution. Having produced such a charter, the framers rightly departed from Philadelphia with the distinct impression that the sun was rising and not setting over America.

The delegates were realists, however. After having spent most of a sweltering Philadelphia summer debating behind the closed doors and sealed windows of Independence Hall, they were well aware the principles embodied in the Constitution would stimulate intense and extended debate in some of the states. Indeed, on September 17, 1787, only thirty-nine of the forty-two delegates in attendance were willing to sign the Constitution. Other respected statesmen had refused to attend the convention, perhaps the most noted being Patrick Henry, the freedom fighter from Virginia, who declined to become involved because he "smelled a rat"—a strong national government. In addition, the delegates had done more than just diverge from the "sole and express" mandate given by the Continental Congress, which had called only for a study of the existing commercial problems and possible amendments to the Articles of Confederation; no one in the Continental Congress had said anything about drafting a document constituting a new form of government.

So when the framers emerged from the convention with the Constitution, they knew the sun was also rising on a period of ratification that would be marked by significant controversy. Indeed, it was far from certain the Constitution would be ratified by the requisite number of states. When asked what the convention had created, Benjamin Franklin replied, "A republic, if you can keep it."

The Federalist Papers were written in this setting. They were drafted by three of the convention's most respected delegates—Alexander Hamilton and John Jay of New York, and James Madison of Virginia—during the ratification battle. The papers were written under the pseudonym "Publius," and the true identity of the authors was not known by the general public for decades. As was common for the era, the authors let their ideas rather than their identities do the talking.

Hamilton, Madison, and Jay wrote *The Federalist Papers* as briefs for those who were debating ratification of the Constitution. They directed their essays at the people of New York and, more specifically, at the delegates who were to attend the New York ratification convention. As such, *The Federalist Papers* were political papers. A New York newspaper published the first of *The Federalist Papers* on October 27, 1787. The authors, primarily Alexander Hamilton, subsequently made sure *The Federalist Papers* were distributed in virtually every state. Madison himself carried copies to the important ratification convention held in Richmond, Virginia.

However, Hamilton, Madison, and Jay undoubtedly wrote *The Federalist Papers* for future generations as well. Martin Diamond and others have observed that the authors of *The Federalist Papers* "looked beyond the immediate struggle and wrote with a view to influencing later generations by making their work the authoritative commentary on the meaning of the Constitution. . . . [*The Federalist*] spoke to thoughtful men then and now, with a view to permanence of its arguments."[1] Plainly the authors were writing on paper views they each had long entertained and wanted to pass on to yet unborn Americans.

Even if the extent to which *The Federalist Papers* contributed to the overall ratification process may be open to question, their subsequent impact in this and other countries is immeasurable. The Constitution sets forth the framework for the dynamic new form of government envisioned by the framers; but *The Federalist Papers* defend the framework, explain it, and fill many of the gaps left open by the charter. And even though the authors themselves certainly did not agree on all of the concepts contained in the eighty-five essays, *The Federalist Papers* elucidate the ideas and logic of three of the men who debated on the floor at Independence Hall; the essays are true constitutional commentaries and represent some of the most persuasive articles ever written about government. Logically, then, *The Federalist Papers* have become valuable tools for judges in interpreting the Constitution.

For example, beginning with the distinguished opinions of John Marshall, the Supreme Court has made clear that the Constitution serves not only as a limit on the powers of the federal government, but also as a guide to their use. When the text of the Constitution is silent or unclear on an issue, especially an issue dealing with the power of the federal government, the Supreme Court often cites *The Federalist Papers* as authority to support its decisions. Over eighty years ago Chief Justice Edward D. White wrote in *Pacific States Telephone and Telegraph Co. v. Oregon* that in ascertaining the meaning of the phrase "Republican Form of Government" found in Section 4 of Article IV of the Constitution, "The debates of the constitutional conventions and the *Federalist Papers* are of great importance, if not conclusive."[2] And, as in *Hines v. Davidowitz*, when analyzing the power of the federal government over areas such as foreign affairs, the Court looks not only at the text of the Constitution, but also to the "authors of the *Federalist Papers*."[3] In short, as Chief Justice William H. Rehnquist recognized in *Dames & Moore v. Regan*, whenever the Court is presented with a question that touches "fundamentally upon the manner in which our Republic is to be governed," it has "the benefit of commentators such as John Jay, Alexander Hamilton, and James Madison writing in the *Federalist Papers* at the Nation's very inception."[4] This is why, in the words of Justice Joseph Story, judges and historians alike view *The Federalist Papers* as "an incomparable commentary of three of the greatest statesmen of their age."[5]

After that long, hot summer in Philadelphia, Alexander Hamilton enlisted the efforts of James Madison and John Jay, and together they wrote *The Federalist Papers* in support of the Constitution. It seems only fitting that in the wake of this nation's celebration of the bicentennial of the Constitution we should read and learn more about these incomparable commentaries which support that great charter.

— **Warren E. Burger**
Chief Justice of the United States (Retired)

Editor's Preface

The origins of this study lie in the period of the Bicentennial of the U.S. Constitution, 1987–91. In a coincidence few could have anticipated, events and observances in honor of this historic document took place at a time of tremendous political upheaval in many parts of the world. Certain questions recurred in conversations with overseas jurists, constitution writers, teachers, and lawyers during that time: How do you govern a society? How do you create a constitution that works—and lasts? One era of dictators and military rulers is passing; but governments with broadly based citizen participation can be fragile institutions, prone, when challenged, to collapse into anarchy, and vulnerable to authoritarian takeovers followed by widespread citizen disenchantment with political life.

In discussions abroad, in meetings with civic leaders from other nations, and in talks in American classrooms, a frequent question was, Why has the American Constitution lasted more than two hundred years? What conceptual and structural features account for its longevity? During the bicentennial period, more than two hundred speakers went abroad to discuss constitutional subjects; the Constitution was distributed in thousands of copies and numerous languages; and law and history books, scholarly conferences, and interactive television programs involving several countries all contributed to the international traffic in constitutional ideas.

The former Chief Justice of the United States, Warren E. Burger, actively participated in these initiatives, often meeting with judges, lawyers, and students, and sharing the bicentennial commission's "history and civics lesson for America" with local and international audiences. Although each country has its unique historical, political, and legal traditions, a preoccupation with fundamental questions of governance is universal, and answering the question, What animated the framers of the Constitution? is useful for both overseas audiences, some of whom struggle with basic questions of political order, and domestic readers, who often venerate, but do not necessarily understand, the Constitution's dynamics.

The Federalist Papers, of course, provide much of the needed information, but not always in easily accessible form. Although of a high literary order and unparalleled as statements of political thought and explanations of the Constitution, they were initially works of advocacy journalism, turned out by skilled writers, often at three- or four-day intervals, to gain the important New York delegation's votes for the Constitution. James Madison wrote that "it frequently happened that whilst the printer was putting into type parts of a number, the following parts were under the pen and to be furnished in time for the press."

Nor do all of the essays written for that specific purpose in the autumn of 1787 and spring of 1788 have lasting relevance. The reasons for the failure of the Articles of Confederation are instructive to read, but are reworked and rewoven several times. Lengthy sections on the shortcomings of Greek and Roman models come close to law office history in places, and there are detailed commentaries on long-solved issues, such as the relationship of local militia to a national standing army. *The Federalist's* case that a national government is advantageous because, among other things, it will be neither large nor costly, does not bear the test of time; nor does the argument that no Bill of Rights is needed because rights are protected adequately throughout the document and by state constitutions.

Nevertheless, the papers belong among the classics of global political thought, and modern readers will recognize the lasting appeal of the twenty-three included in this volume. A brief introduction to each of the papers collected here summarizes the content and clarifies the author's intent. The text of the papers is taken from the McLean edition of 1788, "printed and sold by J. and A. McLean, No. 41, Hanover-Square," with some modernization of spelling, punctuation, and typography. The division of authorship among Alexander Hamilton, John Jay, and James Madison is that established originally by the scholarly detective work of Professor Douglas Adair. A few paragraphs about the deficiencies of ancient republics have been deleted. Subheads have been added to more easily identify the subjects of individual papers. This accommodation for modern readers interrupts the symmetrical, meticulous structure and flow of *The Federalist*, but those who enjoy the original essays' worldview and elegant language can read them through unhindered.

Hamilton's finely honed enthusiasm, Madison's carefully wrought statements about the human condition, *The Federalist's* hopeful vision for the new nation, and its clear arguments not only survive the test of time admirably but provide benchmarks against which future political theorists may measure the efforts of others. Even those with an aversion to hagiography will not contest Clinton Rossiter's statement that "*The Federalist* is the most important work in political science that has ever been written, or is likely to be written, in the United States. It is, indeed, the one product of the American mind that is rightly counted among the classics of political theory."[1]

"The essays were almost as important as the Constitution itself," the American historian Page Smith writes, adding, "In all arguments about the meaning or interpretation of that sometimes obscure document, they have been quoted by political scientists, judges, and lawyers as authoritative."[2] Though acknowledged as advocacy pieces, the U.S. Supreme Court has recognized *The Federalist Papers* to be an important explication of the Constitution, sufficient to impart the framers' objectives.

And so, at a time in world history when countries in Asia, Africa, Latin America, and parts of Europe are reconsidering both the ideas and structures of governance, they will find in Hamilton, Madison, and Jay thoughtful interlocutors. *The Federalist Papers'* authors were keen observers of humanity's destructive tendencies, its hopeful prospects, and the equally important task of translating ideas into practice in the enduring exercise of free people building self-government.

Acknowledgments

The Chief Justice of the United States (Retired), Warren E. Burger; Professor A.E. Dick Howard, White Burkett Miller Professor of Law and Public Affairs at the University of Virginia Law School; and Robert S. Peck, former Judicial Fellow and head of Public Education Programs for the American Bar Association, read and provided valuable comments on the manuscript. I am grateful to them and to Betty Southard Murphy of the Commission on the Bicentennial of the U.S. Constitution; Judge Charles J. Weiner of the Sixth Federal Circuit, Philadelphia, Pennsylvania; Robert A. Goldwin, former Director of Constitutional Studies of the American Enterprise Institute; and Professor John Norton Moore, Walter L. Brown Professor of Law at the University of Virginia for sharing their insights with me over several years. My thanks are due as well to Ann and Van Kirk Reeves of Paris, France; Fred G. Hilkert, M.D.; and Professor John N. Drobek of Washington University Law School, St. Louis, Missouri, for discussions of the law and its larger issues.

I want to thank Professor Eugen Weber, the Joan Palevsky Professor of Modern European History, University of California at Los Angeles, whose pioneering work, *The Western Tradition*, helped place *The Federalist Papers* in a global context; and Ambassador Thomas R. Byrne and Walter J. Shea, Chairman, Eastern Conference of Teamsters, for many interesting conversations on contemporary international political issues.

THE

FEDERALIST:

A COLLECTION

OF

ESSAYS,

WRITTEN IN FAVOUR OF THE

NEW CONSTITUTION,

AS AGREED UPON BY THE FEDERAL CONVENTION.
SEPTEMBER 17, 1787.

IN TWO VOLUMES.

VOL. I.

NEW-YORK:

PRINTED AND SOLD BY J. AND A. M'LEAN,
No. 41, HANOVER-SQUARE.
M,DCC,LXXXVIII.

Introduction

The long coastline was fair prey for foreign invaders. Roads were few, muddy when it rained, dusty otherwise. Transportation was slow and irregular, most dependable by water. The potentially prosperous, primarily agrarian economy was stagnant, owing to the recent eight-year war, and entrepreneurial people were not sure how it would improve. Scattered insurrections flared, and the prospect of angry mobs or unschooled peasants taking the law into their hands threatened whatever form of government the newly independent states selected. The central government was powerless, lacking authority to raise funds or an army, or to administer justice. Politicians debated at length whether the existing government should be patched up, or if there should be a strong president, a president and council with shared powers, or a legislature with most powers vested in it; but the discussions went nowhere.

The confederation's thirteen isolated states were in infrequent contact with one another, except for commerce along the main maritime arteries. Spanish, French, English, and other metallic coins still circulated long after the war; the Continental Congress's money was valueless. "Not worth a continental" was a popular expression. The wartime military leader, George Washington, wrote state governors in 1783 that he feared "the union cannot be of long duration, and everything must very rapidly tend to anarchy and confusion." Thomas Jefferson, then Minister to France, said, "We are the lowest and most obscure of the whole diplomatic tribe." A British cleric said Americans were "a disunited people till the end of time, suspicious and distrustful to each other, they will be divided and subdivided into little commonwealths, or principalities."

These conditions, which America faced two centuries ago, are applicable to many modern nations. *The Federalist Papers,* first published in 1787–88 in the middle of intense debates over what form the new government should take, explain how the authors of the U.S. Constitution arrived at that document. There is a congruence between basic issues of governance raised then in Philadelphia and now in Warsaw, Conakry, Brasilia, and Moscow. The questions are not rhetorical or theoretical, but are fundamental to the formation of a national government to which all citizens can subscribe, and that will endure.

If the American Revolution was a time of political upheaval, the writing and ratification of the U.S. Constitution was no less revolutionary. The Constitution's framers boldly exceeded their mandate to suggest ways of patching up the Articles of Confederation. The ratification debates required the people to decide whether they would adopt an untried form of government or hold on to an ineffectual one that was sure to result in the balkanization of the new nation. The temptation to maintain individual state sovereignty was strong, even though many conceded the necessity of regional defense treaties. If the Anti-Federalists had prevailed, the sketch in *Federalist* No. 2 of the potentially prosperous nation would have remained an exercise in mapmaking. Far from defending the status quo, *The Federalist Papers,* in measured argument, seek support for a revolutionary form of government, unknown in world history to that date.

Fortunately, the *Federalist* authors—Alexander Hamilton, John Jay, and James Madison—wrote their work at a propitious moment in American history. A few years earlier, in the shadow of the war and the British crown, a proposal for a strong central government would not have found acceptance.[1] Nor could such a concept have succeeded during the Age of Jackson, just around the corner. Its republican features, which kept the people somewhat distant from the reins of power, would have been voted down. *The Federalist Papers* thus explain a revolutionary document that faced a hotly contested ratification battle for the political soul of a nation at a critical turning point in its history.[2]

The Federalist Papers reflect the end of an era in America, a chapter that began with the Mayflower Compact of 1620 and the various covenants, declarations, and state constitutions that followed, and culminated in the Declaration of Independence and Constitution. During that period of more than a century and a half, American political thought was formulated and tried, and arguments were rehearsed and refined in press, pulpit, and legislative chamber, often to express opposition to the British crown, but also to give an expanding country a workable government. It was against such a background that *The Federalist Papers* emerged, combining the traits Robert A. Ferguson ascribes to the Constitution: "generic strength, manipulative brilliance, cunning restraint, and practical eloquence."[3]

Despite their length, the papers are remarkably concise—long enough to establish their argument and answer opponents, but free of invective, extraneous commentary, or florid embellishment. *The Federalist Papers'* grounding in eighteenth-century philosophy and economic theory is only tantalizingly suggested in brief sections seeded throughout the essays. We wish for an additional hour of tavern talk with Madison or Hamilton, or a public television interview program tying up loose ends on the origins of their ideas; but the information is not forthcoming. The authors were primarily practitioners rather than theorists, and *The Federalist Papers* were written for a specific purpose: to convince delegates to New York's ratification convention of the value of a particular course of action.

As such, the essays are a radical, revolutionary statement of well-reasoned political thought, carefully moving beyond the central ideas raised by theorists like Hume, Locke, or Montesquieu. Instead of dramatically overthrowing the old order of theory and practice, the Constitution writers, with careful study, took its best features and gave new meaning to them. As works of theory and guides for practice, the essays are more lasting than anything written by Marx, Lenin, Mao, Castro, or Metternich.

The Federalist Papers represent the most long-lived contributions of a golden age of pamphlet literature. It was a time when public service, most leaders believed, was a responsibility mandated by the Deity, and public documents often reflected a literary quality comparable to contemporary sermons or works of science, history, or political or moral thought.[4] Simultaneously there were improvements in the technology and availability of printing presses; the growth of a relatively affluent, lettered audience; and the emergence of urgent and revolutionary issues, like the coming of age of republican political thought and the question of assembling a machinery of government for the polities that had just defeated the British forces and now must govern themselves.

The Articles of Confederation

Had the Articles of Confederation not failed, there would have been no Constitution and no *Federalist Papers*. Two centuries later, it is difficult to imagine the chaotic state of America in the postrevolutionary period. A war had been won, but the eastern seaboard lay vulnerable to potential invaders. The economy was plagued by multiple currencies and tariffs; state governments were bankrupt and ineffectual; and the central government was central in name only. From 1776 to 1787 America was a loose alliance of states governed by the Articles, whose fatal flaw was that power remained with individual states. The central government could neither raise revenues nor enact legislation binding on individual states. The votes of nine of the thirteen states were required to pass laws, and a unanimous vote was necessary to effect any fundamental change in the Articles.

The central government's weakness was intentional; the American settlers had bitterly resented the British crown's power to control commerce and collect taxes. The legislative body created under the Articles was powerless, and there was no executive or judicial branch. Moreover, the thirteen states each had separate political and commercial interests, and the temporary unity forged from a decade of active hostility toward Great Britain failed to produce a national identity. Nine states had navies; seven printed their own currency; most had tariff and customs laws. New York charged duties on ships moving firewood or farm produce to and from neighboring New Jersey and Connecticut. When soldiers remarked, "New Jersey is our country," they echoed the widespread sentiment of other states.

Also contributing to political chaos in the 1780s were the insolvent state governments. Hamilton, in a stinging attack on the Articles, remarked in *Federalist* No. 9 that they encouraged "little, jealous, clashing, tumultuous commonwealths, the wretched nurseries of unceasing discord." Madison had the bankrupt state governments in mind in *Federalist* No.10 when he described the need to "secure the national councils against any danger from . . . a rage for paper money, for an abolition of debts, for an equal division of property, or for any other improper or wicked project." Madison wrote on October 24, 1787, to Jefferson in France that the unstable state legislatures "contributed more to that uneasiness which produced the convention, and prepared the public mind for a general reform, than those which accrued to our national character and interest from the inadequacy of the confederation to its immediate objects."[5]

Toward Philadelphia

Trade disputes festered among the states in this disruptive setting. A commercial quarrel between Maryland and Virginia over an oyster fishery and navigation rights triggered the meeting that produced plans for a constitutional convention. The Maryland and Virginia delegates invited representatives from other states to meet "to take into consideration the trade of the United States." The issue was larger than informal negotiators could solve, and, at a meeting in Annapolis, Maryland, in the fall of 1786 to resolve commercial disputes, Hamilton and Madison urged delegates from the five states present to convoke all thirteen "to meet at Philadelphia on the second Monday in May next, to take into consideration the situation of the United States, to devise such further provisions as shall appear to them necessary to render the Constitution of the Federal Government adequate to the exigencies of the union." Congress endorsed the convention but gave it the limited mandate of recommending revision of the Articles.

A galvanic event that occurred shortly before the convention met was an agrarian debtors' uprising in western Massachusetts, Shays's Rebellion. Daniel Shays, an officer who had served in the Revolution, was an impoverished debtor by the winter of 1786. In an attempt to gain relief from unpaid debts, Shays and over a thousand destitute followers, armed with pitchforks and staves, tried to prevent county courts from sitting. They wanted tax relief, paper money, and the state capital moved westward from Boston. Their attempt to seize a federal arsenal was thwarted by the local militia. Funded by merchants' subscriptions, the rebels then hastily recruited Boston college students. The rebellion's leaders were hunted down in a snowstorm, sentenced to death, then pardoned or given short prison terms.

The event, which was replicated in several western Massachusetts towns, sent shock waves across the states because of who the participants were, how the crisis was handled, and the divisive issues it raised. The uprising influenced the states' decision to support a central government capable of enforcing public order. Many believed that creating a popular democracy with power vested in local authorities invited anarchy, tyranny, or dismemberment of the body politic.

The Constitutional Convention

The country's future form of government was shaped during four months' deliberations beginning in late May 1787. Twelve states named seventy-four delegates to the convention; only fifty-five came to Philadelphia, and some arrived well after a quorum assembled on May 25. The average age of the delegates was forty-two; five were less than thirty years of age. Madison was thirty-six, Hamilton thirty. Thirty-four representatives were trained as lawyers, many others were merchants and planters. About 60 percent had attended college; Princeton, Yale, Harvard, and Columbia were well represented. The delegates came mostly from their states' tidewater regions. They were professionals and property owners, although some ended their lives in penury. A stabilizing force during the deliberations was the presence of George Washington, convention president, war hero, and likely choice for first president of the United States. Another respected figure was eighty-one-year-old Benjamin Franklin, who contributed infrequently, but importantly, to discussions, and who entertained delegates often at his nearby lodgings during the hot Philadelphia summer.

In modern times, it would be unthinkable for more than fifty leaders to spend nearly four months in intense political deliberations without press coverage, media leaks, or detailed copies of speeches and votes made public. Yet the convention agreed to meet secretly and keep no record of votes, allowing issues to evolve and delegates to change positions. Madison's notes, which were not published until 1840, remain the principal source of subsequent information about the proceedings.

The four-month convention produced several compromises that made the Constitution possible. Shortly after the convention opened, the Virginia delegation tabled a proposal creating three distinct branches of government and a national legislature with power to negate and supersede state laws. A dispute flared over Virginia's proposal that membership in both branches of the legislature should be proportionate to a state's population. Fearing a loss of power, smaller states objected, and New Jersey's William Patterson offered a counterproposal, suggesting that states have an equal number of delegates regardless of size—one state, one vote. Alexander Hamilton observed correctly, "It is a contest for power, not for liberty." Roger Sherman of Connecticut then proposed a compromise, later adopted; membership in the Senate would be limited to two senators per state, and membership in the House of Representatives would be relative to population. Additionally, tax bills and revenue measures would originate in the House, where citizens would be represented by a greater number of members.

Once these compromises were reached, the remaining issues—many as potentially significant as the questions already decided— were soon sorted out. Powers to collect taxes, regulate commerce, and support a national army, which had been denied to the Continental Congress in the Articles of Confederation, were included in the Constitution with little opposition.

Although delegates differed on the new government's structural details, they accepted awarding the national government a more powerful role than anything previously contemplated in America. Basically, the government's powers were expanded, the new Constitution became the "supreme law of the land," and the national government was no longer subservient to state governments. It could reach the people directly through laws, courts, administrative agents, and the previously denied power to raise revenues and armies. "The federal and state governments are in fact but different agents and trustees of the people, with different powers and designed for different purposes," Madison wrote in No. 46. There were thus two distinct governments, state and national, derived from the people and responsible to them. The constitutional government was a democratic republic—democratic because the people were represented, republican because there were restraints on what people and government could do.

Madison and his colleagues engineered a solution to a problem plaguing American government at that time. Instead of depending on the states for its lifeblood of power and funds, the new national government reached down and around states directly to the citizenry, establishing both the central government's authority and creating possibilities for perennial tension as well. Individual rights, states' rights, and the intrusions of "big government" would later become substantive issues in American law and politics, especially with the exponential rise in population and the federal government's influence in the late twentieth century.

When mid-September arrived, some tempers were short, but the convention's principal work was done, and several delegates departed. Thirty-nine of the original fifty-five delegates signed the document. Only three delegates declined to endorse it, and four others who opposed it were absent.

Madison's final notes of the historic event state:

> Whilst the last members were signing it, Doctor Franklin, looking towards the President's chair [Washington was the presiding officer], at the back of which a rising sun happened to be painted, observed to a few members near him, that painters had found it difficult to distinguish in their art a rising from a setting sun. I have, said he, often and often in the course of the

session, and the vicissitudes of my hopes and fears as to its issue, looked at that behind the President without being able to tell whether it was rising or setting: but now at length I have the happiness to know that it is a rising and not a setting sun.[6]

With a deft turn of phrase, Gouverneur Morris made it appear consent was unanimous in the document's concluding lines, since at least one representative from each state in attendance signed: "Done in Convention, by unanimous consent of the States present the 17 September." Then, at 4 p.m. that same day, "The Members adjourned to the City Tavern, dined together, and took cordial leave of each other."

Although the prescient Franklin compared the proceedings to a rising sun, the Constitution's fate was uncertain. The slavery issue had been dealt with to the satisfaction of neither northerners nor southerners; inland farmers and pioneers feared the political and commercial power of tidewater planters; and landed interests, like New York's Governor George Clinton, were apprehensive of Congress's taxation powers. Creditable leaders of the revolutionary generation, like Patrick Henry and Samuel Adams, cast a cold eye on the new government's centralized powers, and there was growing sentiment throughout the states for a bill of rights.

In spite of the fact that their deliberations focused on immediate problems, the Constitution writers, in several instances, both showed a keen awareness of historical precedent and realized they were writing for posterity. Madison records Gouverneur Morris: "He came here as a representative of America; he flattered himself he came here in some degree as a Representative of the whole human race; for the whole human race will be affected by the proceedings of this Convention. He wished gentlemen to extend their views beyond the present moment of time; beyond the narrow limits of place."[7]

Hamilton reflected this larger perspective in *Federalist* No. 34:

> We must bear in mind that we are not to confine our view to the present period, but to look forward to remote futurity. Constitutions of civil governments are not to be framed upon a calculation of existing exigencies, but upon a combination of these with the probable exigencies of the ages, according to the natural and tried course of human affairs.

Still, in September 1787 the delegates were not certain their results would last more than a few years. Someone said all they had was a piece of paper and George Washington. They believed the summer's deliberations and compromises had resulted in a practical, workable frame of government, but many were pessimistic. Alexander Hamilton brooded that the Constitution represented "a weak and worthless fabric"; another delegate called it "the Continental Congress in two volumes instead of one."

The delegates' harmonious evening interlude of September 17, 1787, was a brief calm before a yearlong storm of argument over ratification.

An Uncertain Fate

The Constitution was forwarded to the Continental Congress on September 20, three days after being signed. Reaction was mixed; some members of Congress wanted to censure convention delegates for exceeding their mandate. Nevertheless, Congress moved on September 28 to ratify the document. A majority of nine states was required for the Constitution to become law. Convention delegates—skeptical of popular democratic power and of entrenched powerbrokers, who would oppose any centralization of power—had written into the new Constitution's Article 7 that special conventions, not state legislatures, were required for ratification. The Constitution's supporters eschewed popular referendums, believing that special conventions, whose members were thus "refined" or "filtered," in Madison's language, would produce enlightened delegates and assure the Constitution's passage.

But victory was far from certain. Considerable literature was directed against the Constitution, much of it of a high order.[8] Distinguished patriots opposed the document, including Virginia's George Mason, landowner and author of the Virginia Constitution and Bill of Rights, who called George Washington an "upstart surveyor"; and Thomas Paine, who echoed a widespread sentiment: "That government is best which governs least." The Constitution's opponents included well-known patriots, backcountry farmers, small landholders, artisans, and laborers. They resisted a strong presidency, which "squints toward monarchy," and a Congress with powers of taxation, which could "clutch the purse with one hand and wave the sword with the other," as Henry put it. Madison's opponents believed the ideas incorporated in the Constitution were elitist (*aristocratic* was the word used in the 1780s), favoring the ruling elements, owners of businesses and property, and ignoring small farmers, workers, and those at the margins of society.

The lack of a bill of rights was a major issue with opponents and the undecided, as it was with many of the new Constitution's supporters. Historians of a later generation called it "an *Iliad*, or Parthenon, or Fifth Symphony of statesmanship"; but New York's John Lansing said the Constitution was "a triple headed monster, as deep and wicked a conspiracy as ever was invented in the darkest ages against the liberties of a free people." It was against this backdrop that *The Federalist Papers* appeared.

The Name *Federalist*

Proponents of the American Constitution gained a tactical advantage over those who opposed it or had reservations by claiming the name *Federalist* for themselves and by calling opponents *Anti-Federalists*. In the 1780s, partisans of a strong national government were called *nationalists*. Federalists, in contrast, supported state sovereignty and opposed a dominant national government. By preempting the title *Federalist*, Hamilton and his coauthors gained an advantage for their position and avoided an all-out confrontation over the issue of state versus national power. They appeared as supporters of states' rights, a theme elucidated in *The Federalist Papers*, yet were clearly advocates as well of a strong national government.

Publius

The essays were signed "Publius." Classical pseudonyms and allusions to Greek and Roman history were popular with eighteenth-century American authors, and towns across the country were named Athens, Sparta, Rome, and Ithaca. Statues of heroes, like Washington or Jefferson, showed them clad in togas, with Roman features. Hamilton, originator of *The Federalist Papers*, made a shrewd choice in Publius. The name referred to Publius Valerius, the state builder who restored the Roman republic following the overthrow of Tarquin, Rome's last king. Plutarch compared Publius favorably to Solon, Greece's law giver. Now a modern Publius would help build the new American republic.

In selecting a name like Publius, the *Federalist* authors followed a practice common among eighteenth-century public document writers. They published a collaborative work under a pseudonym rather than a byline. If Hamilton, Madison, and Jay had publicized their authorship of

The Federalist Papers, they would have been identified as advocates of particular positions, and they, rather than their arguments, would have become part of the debate over the Constitution. Likewise, if Americans in 1787 had known it was Pennsylvania's aristocratic, conservative Gouverneur Morris who had taken the Constitution's penultimate drafts and composed the final document, it could have diminished chances for ratification. But Morris's anonymity was preserved until the 1830s, as was authorship of *The Federalist Papers* until the 1840s. Hamilton, Madison, and Jay thus upheld a practice common in that era, creating a veil of anonymity that forced readers to focus on arguments rather than authors. This allowed politicians to develop ideas free from public pressures, change their minds during deliberations, and explore differences until conclusions were reached.

Choosing anonymity was also a function of the rivalry between Hamilton and New York Governor George Clinton. Hamilton was the only New York delegate who signed the Constitution. Clinton was an Anti-Federalist leader in a state where those opposing the new Constitution held a commanding majority. Choosing Publius was, in part, an attempt to move the debate away from the strong personal animosity between Hamilton and Clinton.

The Federalist Papers Plan

A modern reader, interested in the papers' core arguments, will be drawn to approximately twenty essays that retain lasting appeal. Their broad categories were enumerated by Hamilton in *Federalist* No. 1, in which he proposes that his plea for union and republicanism be divided clearly into six "branches of inquiry": (1) the "utility of union," (2) "the insufficiency of the present Confederation," (3) the necessity of energetic government, (4) the Constitution's republican nature, (5) its compatibility with state constitutions, and (6) the security it provides both liberty and property.

The series has a careful unity, not always apparent to later readers. The first thirty-seven papers detail shortcomings in the Articles of Confederation. Numbers 2–14 advocate a federal union as opposed to independent states and argue that a large country supports democracy better than a small country, a much-debated issue in the 1780s.

Madison's No. 10, which in modern times has become the best-known single essay, contains his famous definition of faction and his observations on human nature. After an enumeration of the Articles' flaws in Nos. 15–22, Nos. 23–36 make the case for the new government.

The argument for the Constitution is then stated positively in Nos. 37–51. The House of Representatives is described in Nos. 52–61, the Senate in Nos. 62–66, the presidency in Nos. 67–77, and the judiciary, including the principle of judicial review, in Nos. 78–83. Number 84 contends a Bill of Rights is not necessary because rights are provided throughout the Constitution; in No. 85 Hamilton presents an upbeat finale, closing the series on the optimistic note with which it began.

Although the series has a clearly enunciated argument line and organization, certain papers and sections of papers—for example, Nos. 10, 37, 39, 47, 51, 78, and 84—move beyond skilled polemics to a place among the most profound commentaries ever published on human behavior in political society. These include some carefully shaped darker passages about the failure of the Articles of Confederation and humanity's propensity to greed and self-interest, and passages of controlled enthusiasm on future hopes for the young republic.

Even though the papers were turned out quickly and the principal authors represented different viewpoints, they were still the product of careful planning and execution. It was Hamilton's tactical brilliance that saw the need for this comprehensive project. He conceived the idea of writing *The Federalist Papers*, produced the outline, and recruited the writers, deciding against other potential contributors whose attempts at essays he regarded as mediocre. Hamilton and Madison were in close contact for over a year, lived under the failed Articles, and spent the summer of 1787 debating constitutional issues in Philadelphia. The careful reasoning and construction of some papers and sections of others, like Nos. 10 and 51, suggest their authors prepared some arguments in advance and reshaped them for use in the series. Madison could draw on several years' worth of carefully refined notes on earlier experiments in government, the results of long study and reflection.

The writers did not lack subject matter; the challenge was to order arguments convincingly. This took place against a barrage of pamphlets and newspaper commentaries from opponents like "Cato" and "Brutus" and the support of bombastic friends like "Caesar." Still, *The Federalist* authors seized the high ground with a thoughtful format and carefully crafted arguments, avoiding personal attacks and the ambushes and broadsides of traditional political journalism.

Publication: October 27, 1787 – August 15, 1788

The Federalist Papers were originally published to win New York's support for ratification of the Constitution. Ratification was to be decided at a special convention; thus, the essays aimed to influence the delegate selection process by building support for the Federalist candidates for election to the June 1788 convention.

The essays, part of a deluge of pamphlets and newspaper articles for and against the Constitution, first ran in New York's *Independent Journal* on October 27, 1787, and appeared on Wednesdays and Saturdays; on Tuesdays they were printed in another paper, and on Wednesdays and Thursdays in still another publication. When the *New York Journal* began circulating in 1788, it carried them as well. This outpouring extended until the following April, with the publication of No. 77, Hamilton's concluding essay on the presidency. The series resumed on June 17, with the important essays on the judiciary, and continued until August 15, 1788, when the last of the 85 works was published.

The Federalist Papers appeared in book form before the newspaper series ended; Hamilton dispatched them to Madison in Virginia to distribute to that state's delegation prior to its vote on the Constitution. Otherwise, their circulation was confined largely to New York, with scattered printings in Pennsylvania and some New England states. A French edition appeared in 1792, followed in the next two centuries by over a hundred editions or reprints in English and at least twenty foreign language editions. A Portuguese edition was published in Rio de Janeiro in 1840, a condensed German version in Bremen in 1864, and a Spanish edition in Buenos Aires in 1868.

Ironically, a French diplomat, writing in New York in 1788, found *The Federalist* not worth commenting on. It was "of no use to the well-informed, and . . . too learned and too long for the ignorant." A contemporary New York newspaper lamented "the dry trash of Publius in 150 numbers," and "Twenty-Seven Subscribers" protested the *Journal*'s "cramming us with the voluminous Publius," which "has become nauseous, having been served up to us no less than in two other papers on the same day."[9]

Alexander Hamilton arranged for the publication of *The Federalist Papers*. According to popular lore, he wrote *Federalist* No. 1 on board a ship bringing him down the Hudson River from Albany to New York City in early October 1787. He invited Madison to coauthor the series only after other choices either had declined or written unusable essays. Hamilton and Madison were both in New York in the fall of 1787 as congressional delegates and could confer with one another. Hamilton probably wrote Nos. 1, 6–9, 11–13, 15–17, 21–36, 59–61, and 65–85. Madison wrote the important Nos. 10 and 51, and 14, 37–58, and most likely 62–63. Madison and Hamilton may have jointly authored Nos. 18–20. Madison's contributions ended in March 1788 when he returned to Virginia for that state's ratification debates. John Jay, who was originally expected to have a more significant role in the project, became ill during the winter and wrote only five essays, Nos. 2–5 and 64. The authors, although drawn from the political and economic leadership of their time, represented both similarities and differences in viewpoints.

The Authors

Alexander Hamilton (1757–1804) was born on the island of Nevis in the West Indies of a Scottish merchant father and a mother of Huguenot descent. His family origins gave rise to romantic speculation; John Adams, his avowed opponent, called him the "bastard brat of a Scotch peddler." Hamilton entered Columbia University, then called King's College, at age sixteen. During the American Revolution he rose to officer rank and became George Washington's aide-de-camp and private secretary for four years. After the war, Hamilton studied law and practiced successfully in New York, entering Congress in 1782. In addition to originating *The Federalist Papers*, Hamilton was an energetic author on other subjects, having written in support of the Boston patriots and later founding a newspaper in New York. Handsome, intense, aggressive, and self-assured to the point of arrogance, Hamilton married the socially prominent daughter of a rich New York merchant. Hamilton was not an original thinker, but possessed a well-disciplined legal mind, skills in public debate, and an ability to lay issues before the public in a compelling manner. In Washington's cabinet, Hamilton served as secretary of the treasury until 1795, when he resigned to return to the practice of law, remaining a close advisor to Washington until the latter's death. Hamilton was a leader in the Federalist Party and in later years was often in conflict with his coauthor Madison. A proponent of nationalism but not direct democracy, Hamilton once said, "Men are reasoning rather than reasonable animals." This dashing figure, filled with promise, was killed in a duel with Aaron Burr in Weehawken, New Jersey, in 1804.

Hamilton and Madison (1751–1836) were a study in contrasts. Scion of an established Virginia family, Madison was a deliberate, rather than a dramatic, public figure, who counted on his careful preparation, an instinct for politics, and meticulously crafted arguments to carry the day. Ralph Ketchum, biographer of Madison, calls his subject "an ardent revolutionist, resourceful framer of government, clever political strategist, cautious, sometimes ineffectual leader."[10] Madison was raised on a four-thousand-acre tidewater plantation. He later studied at Princeton, where he stayed to tutor in political thought with John Witherspoon, the Scottish pastor, intellectual, and the university's president. Madison was well-read in classical and modern writers on politics and history, had thought long and carefully about the relationship of Protestant Christianity to the state, and knew Latin, Greek, Hebrew, and French. He served in the Continental Congress from 1779 to 1783 and in the House of Representatives from 1789 to 1797. He was Jefferson's secretary of state from 1801 to 1808, and president from 1808 to 1816, after which he retired to his Orange County, Virginia, estate, living there until his death in 1836. He is most remembered in history as principal drafter of the Constitution and the Bill of Rights, although he had argued originally a Bill of Rights was not needed, reasoning that the state and federal constitutions guaranteed individual rights sufficiently.

John Jay (1745–1829) was born into an established New York merchant family. His contribution to *The Federalist Papers* was minimal. Severe rheumatism limited him to writing essays Nos. 2 through 5, and No. 64 on the Senate. Like Hamilton, Jay was a successful lawyer and graduate of King's College. An author of the New York State Constitution, he served as president of the Continental Congress in 1778, as ambassador to Spain, and as secretary for foreign affairs from 1784 to 1789. In 1781 he participated in negotiating the treaty that ended hostilities with Great Britain. Jay became the first chief justice of the United States in 1789, and in 1795 he began the first of two terms as governor of New York. At age fifty-six, he retired from active political life to his Westchester County, New York, estate. Jay was a landowner who believed "the people who own the country ought to govern it."

National Security: The Preeminent Issue

There were several issues in the "great national discussion" of 1787 and 1788 to which *The Federalist Papers* spoke. But the authors began with the

17

threat of external and internal danger, the "safety" of the young republic. With memories of the recent war with Britain fresh and the weakness of the Continental Congress apparent, no issue was more important to the Constitution writers than national security. The Federalists believed only a strong central government could defend the country's borders and promote commerce. Hamilton wrote in No. 34, "Let us recollect that peace or war will not always be left to our option; that however moderate or unambitious we may be, we cannot count upon the moderation, or hope to extinguish the ambition of others." Hamilton spoke in No. 34 of the "fiery and destructive passions of war," which are more prevalent than "the mild and beneficent sentiments of peace." He urged a strong national government to provide defenses the republic lacked, and observed, "To model our political systems upon speculations of lasting tranquility would be to calculate on the weaker springs of the human character."

Democratic Versus Republican Government

Certain key words recur in *The Federalist Papers*. Their use is deceptively simple. At first glance, they appear to be common adjectives and nouns; in reality, they carefully move republican political thought of the time decisively ahead, from episodic theoretical insights to a bold but yet untried plan for governing a new nation. Madison recognized the challenge. His explanation of the inadequacies of political language in No. 37 is more than a philosophical aside:

> Besides the obscurity arising from the complexity of objects, and the imperfection of the human faculties, the medium through which the conceptions of men are conveyed to each other adds a fresh embarrassment. The use of words is to express ideas. When the Almighty himself condescends to address mankind in their own language, his meaning, luminous as it may be, is rendered dim and doubtful by the cloudy medium through which it is communicated.

Here are the essential words. The authors wanted a *robust, energetic,* and *vigorous* government; they regarded *faction* as a great enemy of constitutional government; the dangers of uncontrolled popular government had to be *filtered* and *refined* through republicanism. This was done through "framing a government," Madison wrote in *Federalist* No. 51. *Framing* meant not only defining government's outer limits or parameters, but giving government internal form and cohesion as well.

In the worldview of *The Federalist Papers'* authors, the domains of politics, science, and religion were interwoven, and a graduate of one of the handful of eastern universities would be as conversant about the ideas of reformed Protestantism in politics as about developments in Newtonian physics. *Sphere, body,* and *orbit* are words lifted from eighteenth-century natural science; *The Federalist Papers'* writers move them directly into political literature, suggesting the order the new Constitution will provide.

There is a carefully planned use of political space in *The Federalist Papers*. The compact land described by Jay in No. 2, reminiscent of scenes depicted by early American landscape artists, extends gradually as the Confederation's limited confines are pushed back. By the time a defense of the new Constitution is introduced by Hamilton in No. 23, geographic and conceptual horizons are expanded. Hamilton, less the philosophe and more the power broker than Madison, wants *ample* authority, *ample* power, the *extension* of authority, and resists the idea that "we ought to contract our views." Amplitude as an idea in science, and with it the broadening of conceptual horizons, fit Hamilton's political goal of fashioning a political system to govern "so large an empire."

For the task of constructing a system of government, the Founders drew on Newton's understanding of a universe "moving according to mathematical laws in space and time, under the influence of definite and dependable forces." This concept was illustrated by David Rittenhouse, a Philadelphia scientist-politician and Pennsylvania's treasurer, whose orrery displays the motion of solar bodies through the rotation of metal balls moved by wheelworks.[11]

How can there be effective government that is truly representative of the people and that works in a "robust," "vigorous," "energetic" way? The focal point of the question was the clear division over republican government, with access to power separated and checked at various points in the political system, versus a broadly based popular democracy. Instead of votes under the village tree or in town meetings, with larger councils setting national policy, the Constitution writers were architects of an intricate machine whose structural components included such concepts as separation of powers, checks and balances, federalism, and an independent judiciary with the power of judicial review over the acts of legislative and executive bodies.

There were further barriers to a quick or sustained seizure of power: a bicameral legislature, indirect elections, the presidential veto, legislative control of the budget, and limitations on who was eligible to vote. It was almost impossible for a zealous movement to sweep like wildfire through the structures of government and seize control. Likewise, because the safeguards engineered into the system were so elaborate, almost like mechanical safety devices, it was unlikely a tyrant could seize and hold the government for long. Madison used the words *refine* and *filter* to explain how the process differed from direct democracy. In *Federalist* No. 10 he said republican government would "refine and enlarge the public views by passing them through the medium of a chosen body of citizens whose wisdom may best discern the true interest of their country, and whose patriotism and love of justice will be least likely to sacrifice it to temporary or partial considerations." Here Madison deftly appropriated the word *republican* for a specific use, as had been the case with *Federalist*. Madison's republic was not a popular democracy; in it power was not left directly in the hands of the people but with elected officials, thus providing a protective barrier from impulsive or unwise mob governance.

Jay believed the filtering process produced more enlightened, able candidates for national than for state office. In *Federalist* No. 3 he argued that once an efficient national government was established, "the best men in the country . . . will generally be appointed to manage it." The national government "will have the widest field for choice, and never experience that want of proper persons which is not uncommon in some of the States." *Wisdom, regularity, coolness, temperate, reasonable,* and *deliberate* were words the three authors used to describe the leadership the national government would attract through its filtered and refined selection process. This protected the country against impulsive decisions by uninformed mobs who would put self-interest first, the sort of persons Pennsylvania's Gouverneur Morris described in 1774:

> I stood on the balcony and on my right hand were ranged all the people of property, with some few poor dependents, and on the other the tradesmen, etc., who thought it worth their while to leave daily labour for the good of the country. . . . The mob began to think and reason. Poor reptiles! It is with them a *vernal* morning: they are struggling to cast off their winter's slough. They bask in the sunshine, and ere noon they will bite, depend on it.[12]

Opponents like Patrick Henry and Richard Henry Lee rejected such views as elitist republican rhetoric. Lee wrote, "Every man of reflection must see that the change now proposed is a transfer of power from the many to the few."

The Anti-Federalists favored town meetings, public assemblies, frequent elections, and large legislative bodies—the larger the body, the more representative it was of the general will, an idea borrowed from Rousseau. In such a view, government mirrors, rather than filters, popular interest. Hamilton's opponent, Melancton Smith, articulated this position at the New York ratification convention. Smith believed officials were elected to defend the interests of their constituents; he pleaded for "a sameness . . . between the representative and his constituents." He feared "the middling class of life" would be barred from political participation in the system Madison, Hamilton, and Jay proposed. Madison was no supporter of frequent elections. He used the words *energy* and *stability* to describe government's ideal characteristics; and such government required wise, dispassionate leaders having both distance from constituencies and duration of appointment to represent a national, rather than a local, interest.

The *Federalist* writers, in short, were explicit about the difference between a pure democracy, in which liberty prevails and the people decide all questions, and a republican government, in which powers are carefully delineated and divided among the government's different parts. The shift from liberty to order reflected a transformation from ideas prevalent in America in 1776 to those current in 1787. The *Pennsylvania Packet* in September 1787 wrote, "The year 1776 is celebrated for a revolution in favor of liberty. The year 1787 it is expected will be celebrated with equal joy for a revolution in favor of government."[13] It reflected Alexander Hamilton's argument that in 1776 "zeal for liberty became predominant and excessive," and in 1787 the issue was "strength and stability in the organization of our government, and vigor in its operations."[14]

Hamilton, Madison, and Jay knew the national and state governments' weaknesses. States were debtors, so were individuals. Moreover, the revolutionary period's small circle of educated, purposeful national leaders had been replaced in state legislatures by less able figures. Madison in 1788 said the state governing bodies were filled with "men without reading, experience, or principle." Jay worried about states being governed by people whom "wisdom would have left in obscurity."

Although the Federalists won and the Constitution was accepted, the debate never completely ended; the issues remain two centuries later in appeals to populism or republicanism, state and local rights versus national responsibility.

Who Participates in the Political Process?

The analysis of political society Hamilton sketched favored "landholders, merchants, and men of the learned professions." In No. 35 he argued, "We must therefore consider merchants as the natural representatives of all these classes of the community." Mechanics and manufacturers "will always be inclined . . . to give their votes to merchants in preference to persons of their own professions or trades" because "they know that the merchant is their natural patron and friend." Learned professions "truly form no distinct interest in society." Hamilton acknowledged that his portrait of society was limited to a small circle of land-owning leaders. He deftly sidestepped the issue of popular democracy. "If it should be objected that we have seen other descriptions of men in the local legislatures," he wrote in No. 36, "I answer that it is admitted there are exceptions to the rule, but not in sufficient number to influence the general complexion or character of the government."

Still, the door to upward political, economic, and social mobility was not closed. Hamilton's words were autobiographical: "There are strong minds in every walk of life that will rise superior to the disadvantages of situation and will command the tribute due their merit, not only from the classes to which they particularly belong, but from the society in general."

He concluded, "for the credit of human nature . . . we should see examples of such vigorous plants flourishing in the soil of federal as well as of state legislation," but these will be exceptions.

American constitutional history can be charted by the continuing expansion of the voting franchise. The elimination of property requirements, the Fifteenth, Nineteenth, Twenty-third, Twenty-fourth, and Twenty-sixth amendments, and the Voting Rights Act are all aspects of the growth of suffrage rights.

Parenthetically, the Constitution was not ratified by plebiscite; property requirements for voting eliminated many small farmers and artisans who opposed the document. If the Constitution had been submitted directly to the people for a vote, it probably would not have passed. State constitutional convention delegates were elected on the same basis as delegates to state legislatures, which favored established tidewater interests. Nevertheless, in 1788 the voting franchise was broader than it had been when either the Declaration of Independence or the Articles of Confederation was adopted, and New York expanded its electoral rolls and recognized universal manhood suffrage for the election of delegates to its state ratification convention.

Faction

No question of governance received more of Madison's attention than how to have a vigorous, energetic, effective government without allowing a single majority or minority faction, or combination of interests, to seize control of it. Madison weighed both the aftermath of Shays's Rebellion in the north and the trouble hundreds of southern landowners, farmers, artisans, merchants, debtors, and failed property owners would make if allowed into the political arena as equals. He described the problem in *Federalist* No. 10:

> The most common and durable source of factions has been the various and unequal distribution of property. Those who hold and those who are without property have ever formed distinct interests in society.... creditors ... debtors.... A landed interest, a manufacturing interest, a mercantile interest, a moneyed interest.... The regulation of these various and interfering interests forms the principal task of modern legislation.

Madison believed "all civilized societies" were "divided into different sects, fashions, and interests, as they happened to consist of rich and poor, debtors and creditors, the landed, the manufacturing, the commercial interests, the inhabitants of this district or that district." Enlarge the circle of political participants, he argued, while dividing the community into numerous interests and parties, and it will be increasingly difficult for a special interest group to consolidate power and dominate the country or ignore a minority within the nation.

In discussing faction, Madison foresaw not only a vociferous, intransigent minority, but the dangers a majority, bent on working its will, could wreak on society. It was the great mass of restless, propertyless people and small farmers that the Constitution writers both sought to include in a democracy and control in a republic.

Although *Federalist* No. 10 provides an encompassing statement of Madison's idea of faction, he elaborated on the concept elsewhere. In an October 24, 1787, letter to Jefferson he wrote, "*Divide et imperia,* the reprobated axiom of tyranny, is, under certain qualifications the only policy by which a republic can be administered on just principles."[15] Four months earlier, in a speech to the Constitutional Convention, he described his ideas in greater detail. The problem: to have a working republican government yet protect minority interests. This can only be done if government is

> to enlarge the sphere and thereby divide the community into
> so great a number of interests and parties, that in the first place
> a majority will not be likely at the same moment to have a
> common interest separate from that of the whole or of the
> minority; and in the second place, that in case they should have
> such an interest, they may not be apt to unite in pursuit of it. It
> was incumbent on us then to try this remedy, and with that view
> to frame a republican system on such a scale and in such a form
> as will control all the evils which have been experienced.[16]

Madison, in short, faced a balancing act; and a misformulation could tilt the new government, so full of hope and promise, into the hands of an authoritarian president, or worse, a tyrant, or an equally oppressive legislative body. In Madison's view, government was a framework, a mechanical structure to keep political currents within acceptable limits, as a carefully engineered watercourse contains raging streams. Madison was much like Locke in this regard and saw government as a neutral agent brokering competing interests, an umpire among contending forces, an agent to protect property rights, on which the well-being of the fragile new nation rested.

Separation of Powers

After the Revolution, Americans understandably opposed conferring political power on a strong ruler. The memory of George III was fresh, and a much more attractive prospect was a strong legislature. The Constitution failed to award such concentrated power to the legislature. Instead, it created a strong presidency, but power was shared among the executive, legislative, and judicial branches; within the legislative branch, it was further partitioned between two houses. Madison believed the new political system could be wrecked easily by an imbalance in the distribution of power or its concentration in one place, especially in the legislature. In *Federalist* No. 47 he wrote, "The accumulation of all powers, legislative, executive, and judiciary, in the same hands ... may justly be pronounced the very definition of tyranny."

The only reason such a powerful presidency was approved was because everyone knew George Washington would be the first president and would set a clear precedent for how the office should be conducted. Congress, too, would be a strong institution, every bit as capable of despotic rule as the presidency. Madison wrote of the legislature's tendency to draw everything into its vortex; Jefferson earlier had said 173 legislators could be as dictatorial as 1. A strong counterweight in the presidency was important for that reason as well.

Thus the raw confrontation of power against power, ambition against ambition, was counteracted, not through any assumption of goodwill on the participants' part, but through a clear process of separation of powers, distinct checks and balances, and an independent judiciary with the power of judicial review (the right to initiate review of the constitutionality of any act undertaken by the legislative or executive branches, as well as state laws). Judges could face impeachment proceedings in Congress and, while appointed by the president, would be subject to confirmation hearings and sometimes rejection by the Congress.

Madison wrote, in one of the most often-quoted passages from the eighty-five essays, "What is government itself, but the greatest of all reflections on human nature? If men were angels no government would be necessary." Thus, "ambition must be made to counteract ambition"; the government must establish "a policy of supplying by opposite and rival interests, the defect of better motives." Madison's intent was clear: to create a governmental structure in which interests would vigorously contend but not obliterate one another. Elsewhere in No. 51 he stated, "Comprehending in the society so many separate distinctions of citizens . . . will render an unjust combination of a majority of the whole very improbable, if not impracticable."

The Presidency

It was in the presidency that the "energy" and "vigor" of the new republic fused. Hamilton devoted Nos. 67–77 to the presidency. In *Federalist* No. 70 he wrote, "Energy in the executive is a leading character in the definition of good government. . . . A feeble executive implies a feeble execution of the government. A feeble execution is but another phrase for a bad execution: and a government ill executed, whatever it may be in theory, must be, in practice, a bad government."

The president was given powers to veto laws made by Congress; a two-thirds vote of both houses was required to override the veto. The president was, likewise, commander in chief of the armed forces, but Congress declared war and financed the military. The chief executive could conduct foreign affairs, make treaties, and appoint federal judges with the "advice and consent" of the Senate, and pardon those who commit crimes against the nation. What emerged from the convention was a strong presidency, which opponents believed had "powers exceeding those of the most despotic monarch we know of in modern times."[17] Still, presidential power was both separate from legislative and judicial power, and checked and balanced in numerous ways carefully structured into the basic law by Madison and his contemporaries. For example, a president could be impeached for "treason, bribery, or other high crimes and misdemeanors."

Congress

The *Federalist* authors were careful to delineate the powers of Congress, bearing in mind the legislature was the principal governing body in the states. This would not be the case in the new national government. Still, many of the powers given Congress by the Articles were transferred wholesale to the Constitution, including the right to borrow money, declare war, maintain an army and navy, and establish a post office and post roads. In addition, Congress could "lay and collect taxes," regulate commerce with foreign nations and among the states, and invoke the so-called "elastic clause," expanding congressional powers "to make all laws which shall be necessary and proper for carrying into execution the foregoing powers."

The Judiciary

The Constitution and *The Federalist Papers* presented a radically new concept of an independent judiciary with, implicitly, the right to rule on the constitutionality of actions originated by the executive and legislative branches and by state governments. An independent judiciary would only work if judges were given long-term appointments "during good behavior." The judiciary was seen, in No. 78, as having "neither force nor will but merely judgment." Hamilton argued that an independent judiciary was essential to a creditable government because "no man can be sure that he may not be tomorrow the victim of a spirit of injustice, by which he may be a gainer today."

The judiciary's authority to nullify unconstitutional state laws did not come until this century. The Framers did not anticipate this, and the First

Congress rejected a Madison amendment that would have applied certain fundamental rights to state governments as part of the Bill of Rights. Once this power was vested in the judiciary, Justice Oliver Wendell Holmes was the first to note that it was probably more critical to the preservation of liberty than the authority to declare federal actions unconstitutional.

Ratification

When the first *Federalist* paper appeared in print in New York on October 27, 1787, the outcome of the ratification debates was still uncertain. There was widespread opposition, and the Constitution passed by only a narrow margin in several states. John Adams believed "the Constitution was extorted from a reluctant people by a grinding necessity."

Delaware was the first state to accept the Constitution by a unanimous vote on December 7, 1787, and Pennsylvania followed a week later by a margin of 46 to 23. In late December, New Jersey's convention ratified the document unanimously. Georgia ratified the document on January 2, 1788, as did Connecticut by a wide margin seven days later.

In early February the Constitution passed by a vote of 187 to 168 in Massachusetts, following a month of acrimonious debate. Twenty-nine of the 355 delegates meeting in Boston had fought with Captain Shays; many of them urged that the Constitution be sent to the towns for a vote. One of the Massachusetts delegates expressed opponents' fears of a strong central government:

> These lawyers and men of learning, and moneyed men, that talk so finely, and gloss over matters so smoothly, to make us poor illiterate people swallow down the pill, expect to get into Congress themselves; they expect to be managers of this Constitution, and get all the power and all the money into their own hands, and then they will swallow up all us little folks like the great *Leviathan*; yes, just as the whale swallowed up Jonah.[18]

Massachusetts ratified the Constitution, but proposed adding a bill of rights. The proposals were not binding, but they removed the Constitution's supporters from a nettlesome dilemma. The proposals secured votes needed for passage and preserved the flexibility to deal with rights issues reflectively in the drafting room rather than as an up-or-down vote in a public assembly. Many undecided or moderately Anti-Federalist voters were thus willing to give the document a chance.

Three states followed Massachusetts in quick succession with clear majority votes: Maryland in April, South Carolina in May, and New Hampshire in June. They gave the Constitution the needed votes for passage and authorized the formation of a new government.

Meanwhile, several important states, representing about 40 percent of the population, were not heard from, including Virginia, New York, North Carolina, and mercurial Rhode Island. The Virginia and New York votes were crucial if the Constitution was to gain national acceptance. In late June 1788, Virginia voted 89 to 79 to ratify the Constitution, ending a lengthy debate. Madison's presence at the Virginia deliberations was important in gaining the votes needed to support the Constitution. The Richmond contest pitted Madison against Patrick Henry, the colorful orator and patriot who spoke against the document for seven hours one day. Henry's effort, and that of the other Anti-Federalists, eventually resulted in a bill of rights—the first ten amendments to the Constitution—being added to the document. Henry, articulate in debate, was gracious in defeat. "I will be a peaceable citizen," he said. "My head, and my heart, shall be at liberty to retrieve the loss of liberty, and remove the defects of the system in a constitutional way."[19]

"One shudders to think what would have happened had Patrick Henry prevailed in Richmond," Warren E. Burger has written. "Earlier, there had been close votes in Massachusetts and New Hampshire in favor of ratification; Rhode Island had emphatically rejected it by popular referendum. With the Anti-Federalist views of Governor Clinton leading the opposition, sentiment in New York was sharply divided."[20]

New York was pivotal. The national capital and an important commercial center, it was also a geographic link between the nation's two halves. Governor Clinton, like other important New York landowners, opposed the Constitution, fearing both increased taxes and the loss of the state's profitable customs revenues to the national government. In a courthouse in Poughkeepsie during June and July 1788, delegates debated the issues raised in *The Federalist Papers* and at other ratification conventions. As had been the case with Madison in Virginia, Hamilton's spirited participation in the New York debate was crucial. News of the New Hampshire and Virginia votes endorsing the Constitution finally left New York's Anti-Federalists in disarray. On July 26, the New York convention approved the Constitution by a vote of 30 to 27.

That same month North Carolina rejected the proposed law but overturned the vote a year later. Rhode Island, which had not bothered to send a delegation to the Constitutional Convention, finally approved the document 34 to 32 in late May 1790, giving the United States a Constitution ratified by all the states.

It was time now to celebrate. There were parades and civic dinners in major cities; federal punch was a favorite drink, and federal hats were popular. Some parades included a horse-drawn replica of a ship; "The sloop of Anarchy has gone ashore on the rock of Union," read one banner.

Congress accepted the newly ratified Constitution. States sent presidential electors, senators, and representatives to New York, the temporary capital. The new House of Representatives and Senate both organized in March 1789, and George Washington was elected first president; but it took an additional week for the news from New York to reach Washington at his home in Virginia. After a triumphal carriage ride north, Washington took the oath of office on April 30 in New York, reciting the words spelled out in Article II, clause 7, that presidents have used for two centuries: "I do solemnly swear that I will faithfully execute the office of President of the United States and will, to the best of my ability, preserve, protect, and defend the Constitution of the United States."

The Bill of Rights was introduced by Madison in the House of Representatives on June 8, 1789, and approved by Congress on September 25. As approved, the Bill of Rights was part of a series of constitutional amendments Madison introduced. Not all were accepted by the House, and those that were passed were reformulated as an appendix to the Constitution rather than interlarded into the text. The Senate did not approve all of them either, sending twelve of the proposals to the states. Ratification took until December 15, 1791, when Virginia's favorable vote made ten of the twelve proposed amendments part of the Constitution.

The Commercial Republic

The new American experiment in government worked both because the Constitution was a practical, workable document, and because it was launched in an economically viable country. Hamilton, Madison, and Jay realized the importance of a strong commercial republic, although *The Federalist Papers* contain few expanded references to this subject. One of the most detailed was written by Hamilton in *Federalist* No. 12:

> The prosperity of commerce is now perceived and acknowledged by all enlightened statesmen to be the most useful as well as the most productive source of national wealth, and has

accordingly become a primary object of their political cares. By multiplying the means of gratification, by promoting the introduction and circulation of the precious metals, those darling objects of human avarice and enterprise, it serves to vivify and invigorate all the channels of industry and to make them flow with greater activity and copiousness.

"If we mean to be a commercial people," Hamilton argued in *Federalist* No. 24, the nation must have an army and navy. In No. 6, he described the darker side of commercial life in language not unlike that which Madison employed: "Are there not aversions, predilections, rivalships, and desires of unjust acquisitions that affect nations as well as kings? Are not popular assemblies frequently subject to the impulses of rage, resentment, jealousy, avarice, and of other irregular and violent propensities?"

In *Federalist* No. 11, Hamilton was lyrical about "what this country can become." Led by a "vigorous national government, the natural strength and the resources of the country, directed to a common interest, would baffle all the combinations of European jealousy to restrain our growth." Europe would cease being "mistress of the world," America would be the dominant political-economic presence. Hamilton disputed those who argued "that even dogs cease to bark after having breathed awhile in our atmosphere" and described "the adventurous spirit, which distinguishes the commercial character of America." He asserted in No. 12 that in such a republic "the assiduous merchant, the laborious husbandman, the active mechanic, and the industrious manufacturer . . . look forward with eager expectation and growing alacrity to this pleasing reward of their toils."

The Informing Vision

The Founders were in the direct tradition of David Hume and other figures of the Scottish Enlightenment as well as English republican theorists who opposed arbitrary rule and supported popular sovereignty.[21] The great question was one of balance—how to create a strong, acceptable, workable government while avoiding the pitfalls of mob rule or despotism. The Founders' dilemma was expressed by a New England clergyman, Jeremy Belknap: "Let it stand as a principle that government originates from the people: but let the people be taught . . . that they are not able to govern themselves."[22]

The Constitution writers knew Jean Calvin's views on the easy corruptibility of human nature. A seaport town trader or general practicing attorney was rarely a starry-eyed idealist, but was often a person with a clear idea of what was required for honest, workable government, even if such hopes were not always realized. Richard Hofstadter described the Founders' outlook: "Having seen human nature on display in the market place, the courtroom, the legislative chamber, and in every secret path and alleyway where wealth and power are courted, they felt they knew it in all its frailty."[23]

There is a distinctly moral, but not sectarian, cast to *The Federalist Papers*. The authors described "malignant passions" and the "disease," "defect," and "evil propensity" of human behavior in political society. Madison's moralism was evident in the somber analysis of human nature in *Federalist* No. 37. He depicted both "the obscurity arising from the complexity of objects" and "the imperfection of the human faculties." The world is a place with "dark and degraded pictures which display infirmities and depravities of the human character." "Discordant opinions" clash, as do "mutual jealousies ... factions, contentions, and disappointments." On the positive side, he expressed "wonder" and "astonishment" at the constitutional convention's achievement and suggested only "a finger of that Almighty hand" could give mortals adequate understanding to produce a Constitution governing an unruly citizenry.

No influence on the Constitution writers was more important than the Scottish Common Sense school of philosophy. Authors like David Hume, James Harrington, and John Locke acknowledged both the theology of Calvin and the realities of human nature, especially as displayed in the ferment of mid-eighteenth-century Scottish religious, political, and economic councils. John Dickinson, representing Delaware, echoed this viewpoint: "Experience must be our only guide; reason may mislead us." By "reason" he meant the political theory of the Enlightenment. Madison, author of much of the Constitution, was taken with Montesquieu's idea of the separation of powers expressed in the French writer's *Esprit des Lois*; but what made the concept of checks and balances acceptable to the delegates was probably less political theory than economic practice, the desire, expressed in a modern idiom, "to play the game on a level playing field." The Founders' view of human nature was optimistic, but vigilant. "You trust your mother, but you cut the cards," in more recent language.

Madison was an Anglican who had studied with a Presbyterian tutor, John Witherspoon. The problem of morality in public life was central to the

Virginian's thought, more so than personal piety. Ketchum calls Madison's beliefs "eclectic, sensible, and reasonable, if not always wholly consistent," containing "realism about human nature, a comprehensive concept of political obligation, and an instinctive admiration for . . . moderation. From the Christian tradition he inherited a sense of the prime importance of conscience, a strict personal morality, an understanding of human dignity as well as depravity, and a conviction that vital religion could contribute importantly to the general welfare."[24]

The Summing Up

The contrast between the Articles of Confederation and the Constitution and the two ideas of government they represented is evident in the preambles to the two documents. The first was rambling: "To all to whom these presents shall come, we, the undersigned, delegates of the states affixed to our names, send greetings." The second was focused: "We the People of the United States, in Order to form a more perfect Union, establish Justice, insure domestic Tranquility, provide for the common defence, promote the general Welfare, and secure the Blessings of Liberty to ourselves and our Posterity, do ordain and establish this Constitution for the United States of America." In short, the difference was between a bankrupt, ineffectual effort at governance, built on some useful ideas but held together only with the dry sticks of rhetoric, and a bold new plan that balanced popular participation with numerous constraints on what forms that participation might take.

Instead of choosing to locate all political power and ideology in one place, the new idea of government balanced passion against passion, power against power, and harnessed them in an active political process. This is part of what was behind *The Federalist Papers'* studied description of "vigorous," "robust," "energetic" government.

Not often do political essays endure beyond their appointed moment; even more rarely does a lengthy collection of such works, fired off in the heat of polemical politics, claim any lasting place in literary tradition. *The Federalist Papers* endure because the debate is of an unusually high order, about fundamental questions of how society should be governed, by participants who were major actors in shaping the new government.

George Washington signaled the lasting quality of *The Federalist Papers* in a letter to Hamilton on August 28, 1788:

When the transient circumstances and fugitive performances which attended this Crisis shall have disappeared, That Work will merit the Notice of Posterity; because in it are candidly and ably discussed the principles of freedom and the topics of government, which will be always interesting to mankind so long as they shall be connected in Civil Society.[25]

The Federalist

Addressed to the People of the State of New York

No. 1

Introduction

Alexander Hamilton describes the series. He asks the basic question, "whether societies of men are really capable or not of establishing good government from reflection and choice, or whether they are forever destined to depend for their political constitutions on accident and force." Next, he addresses the importance of containing political passion and protecting society from despots who emerge in the guise of proclaiming "zeal for the rights of the people." Hamilton makes a positive case for the new Constitution: "I am convinced that this is the safest course for your liberty, your dignity, and your happiness." He then states The Federalist Papers' *main arguments, which will unfold in eighty-five essays: the advantages of union to political prosperity, the present Confederation's weakness, how the Constitution will provide a structure where "the true principles of republican government" can flourish, its compatibility with state constitutions, and how the Constitution will contribute to the new country's security through safeguarding liberty and property.*

After an unequivocal experience of the inefficacy of the subsisting federal government, you are called upon to deliberate on a new Constitution for the United States of America. The subject speaks its own importance; comprehending in its consequences nothing less than the existence of the Union the safety and welfare of the parts of which it is composed, the fate of an empire in many respects the most interesting in the world. It has been frequently remarked that it seems to have been reserved to the people of this country, by their conduct and example, to decide the important question, whether societies of men are really capable or not of establishing good government from reflection and choice, or whether they are forever destined to depend for their political constitutions on accident and force. If there be any truth in the remark, the crisis at which we are arrived may with propriety be regarded as the era in which that decision is to be made; and a wrong election of the part we shall act may, in this view, deserve to be considered as the general misfortune of mankind.

This idea will add the inducements of philanthropy to those of patriotism, to heighten the solicitude which all considerate and good men must feel for the event. Happy will it be if our choice should be directed by a judicious estimate of our true interests, unperplexed and unbiased by considerations not connected with the public good. But this is a thing more ardently to be wished than seriously to be expected. The plan offered to our deliberations affects too many particular interests, innovates upon too many local institutions, not to involve in its discussion a variety of objects foreign to its merits, and of views, passions, and prejudices little favorable to the discovery of truth.

Among the most formidable of the obstacles which the new Constitution will have to encounter may readily be distinguished the obvious interest of a certain class of men in every State to resist all changes which may hazard a diminution of the power, emolument, and consequence of the offices they hold under the State establishments; and the perverted ambition of another class of men, who will either hope to aggrandize themselves by the confusions of their country, or will flatter themselves with fairer prospects of elevation from the subdivision of the empire into several partial confederacies than from its union under one government.

It is not, however, my design to dwell upon observations of this nature. I am well aware that it would be disingenuous to resolve indiscriminately the opposition of any set of men (merely because their situations might subject them to suspicion) into interested or ambitious views. Candor will oblige us to admit that even such men may be actuated by upright intentions; and it cannot be doubted that much of the opposition which has made its appearance, or may hereafter make its appearance, will spring from sources, blameless at least if not respectable—the honest errors of minds led astray by preconceived jealousies and fears. So numerous indeed and so powerful are the causes which serve to give a false bias to the judgment, that we, upon many occasions, see wise and good men on the wrong as well as on the right side of questions of the first magnitude to society. This circumstance, if duly attended to, would furnish a lesson of moderation to those who are ever so thoroughly persuaded of their being in the right in any controversy. And a further reason for caution, in this respect, might be drawn from the reflection that we are not always sure that those who advocate the truth are influenced by purer principles than their antagonists. Ambition, avarice, personal animosity, party opposition, and many other motives not more laudable than these, are apt to operate as well upon those who support as those who oppose the right side of a question. Were there not even these inducements to moderation, nothing could be more ill-judged than that intolerant spirit which has at all times character- ized political parties. For in politics, as in religion, it is equally absurd to aim at making proselytes by fire and sword. Heresies in either can rarely be cured by persecution.

Guarding Against Despots

And yet, however just these sentiments will be allowed to be, we have already sufficient indications that it will happen in this as in all former cases of great national discussion. A torrent of angry and malignant passions will be let loose. To judge from the conduct of the opposite parties, we shall be led to conclude that they will mutually hope to evince the justness of their opinions, and to increase the number of their converts by the loudness of their declamations and by the bitterness of their invectives. An enlightened zeal for the energy and efficiency of government will be stigmatized as the offspring of a temper fond of despotic power and hostile to the principles of liberty. An over-scrupulous jealousy of danger to the rights of the people, which is more commonly the fault of the head than of the heart, will be represented as mere pretense and artifice, the stale bait for popularity at the expense of public good. It will be forgotten, on the one hand, that jealousy is the usual concomitant of violent love, and that the noble enthusiasm of liberty is too apt to be infected with a spirit of narrow and illiberal distrust. On the other hand, it will be equally forgotten that the vigor of government is essential to the security of liberty; that, in the contemplation of a sound and well-informed judgment, their interests can never be separated; and that a dangerous ambition more often lurks behind the specious mask of zeal for the rights of the people than under the forbidding appearance of zeal for the firmness and efficiency of government. History will teach us that the former has been found a much more certain road to the introduc- tion of despotism than the latter, and that of those men who have overturned the liberties of republics, the greatest number have begun their career by paying an obsequious court to the people, commencing demagogues and ending tyrants.

In the course of the preceding observations, I have had an eye, my fellow-citizens, to putting you upon your guard against all attempts, from whatever quarter, to influence your decision in a matter of the utmost moment to your welfare by any impressions other than those which may result from the evidence of truth. You will, no doubt, at the same time have collected from the general scope of them that they proceed from a source not unfriendly to the new Constitution. Yes, my countrymen, I own to you that after having given it an attentive consideration, I am clearly of opinion it is your interest to adopt it. I am convinced that this is the safest course for your liberty, your dignity, and your happiness. I affect not reserves which I do not feel. I will not amuse you with an appearance of deliberation when I have decided. I frankly acknowledge to you my convictions, and I will freely lay before you the reasons on which they are founded. The consciousness of good intentions disdains ambiguity. I shall not, however, multiply professions on this head. My motives must remain in the depository of my own breast. My arguments will be open to all and may be judged of by all. They shall at least be offered in a spirit which will not disgrace the cause of truth.

The Proposal

I propose, in a series of papers, to discuss the following interesting particulars:—*The utility of the Union to your political prosperity*—*The insufficiency of the present Confederation to preserve that Union*—*The necessity of a government at least equally energetic with the one proposed to the attainment of this object*—*The conformity of the proposed Constitution to the true principles of republican government*—*Its analogy to your own State constitution*—and lastly, *The additional security which its adoption will afford to the preservation of that species of government, to liberty, and to property.*

In the progress of this discussion I shall endeavor to give a satisfactory answer to all the objections which shall have made their appearance, that may seem to have any claim to your attention.

It may perhaps be thought superfluous to offer arguments to prove the utility of the Union, a point, no doubt, deeply engraved on the hearts of the great body of the people in every State, and one which, it may be imagined, has no adversaries. But the fact is that we already hear it whispered in the private circles of those who oppose the new Constitution, that the thirteen States are of too great extent for any general system, and that we must of necessity resort to separate confederacies of distinct portions of the whole. This doctrine will, in all probability, be gradually propagated, till it has votaries enough to countenance an open avowal of it. For nothing can be more evident to those who are able to take an enlarged view of the subject than the alternative of an adoption of the new Constitution or a dismemberment of the Union. It will therefore be of use to begin by examining the advantages of that Union, the certain evils, and the probable dangers, to which every State will be exposed from its dissolution. This shall accordingly constitute the subject of my next address.

No. 2

Concerning Dangers from Foreign Force and Influence

John Jay states that whenever and however government is instituted, "the people must cede to it some of their natural rights, in order to vest it with requisite powers." America's geography favors union, he believes ("Providence has in a particular manner blessed it with a variety of soils and productions and watered it with innumerable streams for the delight and accommodation of inhabitants"), although the Articles of Confederation failed to achieve this union. Jay applauds the recently completed Philadelphia convention's work. The convention met "in the mild season of peace, with minds unoccupied by other subjects." The result is the Constitution, which delegates are now asked to ratify, for "the rejection of it would put the continuance of the Union in the utmost jeopardy." This sober theme is stated throughout The Federalist Papers: *the alternative to the system of government being proposed is weakness before other nations, anarchy within, and a political climate favoring self-interest and regional focus to the detriment of the whole society's security.*

When the people of America reflect that they are now called upon to decide a question, which in its consequences must prove one of the most important that ever engaged their attention, the propriety of their taking a very comprehensive, as well as a very serious, view of it will be evident.

Nothing is more certain than the indispensable necessity of government; and it is equally undeniable that whenever and however it is instituted, the people must cede to it some of their natural rights, in order to vest it with requisite powers. It is well worthy of consideration, therefore, whether it would conduce more to the interest of the people of America that they should, to all general purposes, be one nation, under one federal government, than that they should divide themselves into separate confederacies and give to the head of each the same kind of powers which they are advised to place in one national government.

It has until lately been a received and uncontradicted opinion that the prosperity of the people of America depended on their continuing firmly united, and the wishes, prayers, and efforts of our best and wisest citizens have been constantly directed to that object. But politicians now appear who insist that this opinion is erroneous, and that instead of looking for safety and happiness in union, we ought to seek it in a division of the States into distinct confederacies or sovereignties. However extraordinary this new doctrine may appear, it nevertheless has its advocates; and certain characters who were much opposed to it formerly are at present of the number. Whatever may be the arguments or inducements which have wrought this change in the sentiments and declarations of these gentlemen, it certainly would not be wise in the people at large to adopt these new political tenets without being fully convinced that they are founded in truth and sound policy.

Geography Favors Union

It has often given me pleasure to observe that independent America was not composed of detached and distant territories, but that one connected, fertile, widespreading country was the portion of our western sons of liberty. Providence has in a particular manner blessed it with a variety of soils and productions and watered it with innumerable streams for the delight and accommodation of its inhabitants. A succession of navigable waters forms a kind of chain round its borders, as if to bind it together; while the most noble rivers in the world, running at convenient distances, present them with highways for the easy communication of friendly aids and the mutual transportation and exchange of their various commodities.

With equal pleasure I have as often taken notice that Providence has been pleased to give this one connected country to one united people—a people descended from the same ancestors, speaking the same language, professing the same religion, attached to the same principles of govern-ment, very similar in their manners and customs, and who, by their joint counsels, arms, and efforts, fighting side by side throughout a long and bloody war, have nobly established their general liberty and independence.

This country and this people seem to have been made for each other, and it appears as if it was the design of Providence that an inheritance so proper and convenient for a band of brethren, united to each other by the strongest ties, should never be split into a number of unsocial, jealous, and alien sovereignties.

Similar sentiments have hitherto prevailed among all orders and denominations of men among us. To all general purposes we have uniformly been one people: each individual citizen everywhere enjoying the same national rights, privileges, and protection. As a nation we have made peace and war; as a nation we have vanquished our common enemies; as a nation we have formed alliances, and made treaties, and entered into various compacts and conventions with foreign states.

A strong sense of the value and blessings of union induced the people, at a very early period, to institute a federal government to preserve and perpetuate it. They formed it almost as soon as they had a political existence; nay, at a time when their habitations were in flames, when many of their citizens were bleeding, and when the progress of hostility and desolation left little room for those calm and mature inquiries and reflections which must ever precede the formation of a wise and well-balanced government for a free people. It is not to be wondered at that a government instituted in times so inauspicious should on experiment be found greatly deficient and inadequate to the purpose it was intended to answer.

Arguments for a Strong National Government

This intelligent people perceived and regretted these defects. Still continuing no less attached to union than enamored of liberty, they observed the danger which immediately threatened the former and more remotely the latter; and being persuaded that ample security for both could only be found in a national government more wisely framed, they, as with one voice, convened the late convention at Philadelphia to take that important subject under consideration.

This convention, composed of men who possessed the confidence of the people, and many of whom had become highly distinguished by their patriotism, virtue, and wisdom, in times which tried the minds and hearts of men, undertook the arduous task. In the mild season of peace, with minds unoccupied by other subjects, they passed many months in cool, uninterrupted, and daily consultation; and finally, without having been awed by power, or influenced by any passions except love for their country, they presented and recommended to the people the plan produced by their joint and very unanimous councils.

Admit, for so is the fact, that this plan is only *recommended*, not imposed, yet let it be remembered that it is neither recommended to *blind* approbation, nor to *blind* reprobation; but to that sedate and candid consideration which the magnitude and importance of the subject demand, and which it certainly ought to receive. But, as has been already remarked, it is more to be wished than expected that it may be so considered and examined. Experience on a former occasion teaches us not to be too sanguine in such hopes. It is not yet forgotten that well-grounded apprehensions of imminent danger induced the people of America to form the memorable Congress of 1774. That body recommended certain measures to their constituents, and the event proved their wisdom; yet it is fresh in our memories how soon the press began to teem with pamphlets and weekly papers against those very measures. Not only many of the officers of government, who obeyed the dictates of personal interest, but others, from a mistaken estimate of consequences, from the undue influence of ancient attachments or whose ambition aimed at objects which did not correspond with the public good, were indefatigable in their endeavors to persuade the people to reject the advice of that patriotic Congress. Many, indeed, were deceived and deluded, but the great majority of the people reasoned and decided judiciously; and happy they are in reflecting that they did so.

They considered that the Congress was composed of many wise and experienced men. That, being convened from different parts of the country, they brought with them and communicated to each other a variety of useful information. That, in the course of the time they passed together in inquiring into and discussing the true interests of their country, they must have acquired very accurate knowledge on that head. That they were individually interested in the public liberty and prosperity, and therefore that it was not less their inclination than their duty to recommend only such measures as, after the most mature deliberation, they really thought prudent and advisable.

These and similar considerations then induced the people to rely greatly on the judgment and integrity of the Congress; and they took their advice notwithstanding the various arts and endeavors used to deter and dissuade them from it. But if the people at large had reason to confide in the men of that Congress, few of whom had been fully tried or generally known, still greater reason have they now to respect the judgment and advice of the convention, for it is well known that some of the most distinguished members of that Congress, who have been since tried and justly approved for patriotism and abilities, and who have grown old in acquiring political information, were also members of this convention, and carried into it their accumulated knowledge and experience.

It is worthy of remark that not only the first, but every succeeding Congress, as well as the late convention, have invariably joined with the people in thinking that the prosperity of America depended on its Union. To preserve and perpetuate it was the great object of the people in forming that convention, and it is also the great object of the plan which the convention has advised them to adopt. With what propriety, therefore, or for what good purposes, are attempts at this particular period made by some men to depreciate the importance of the Union? Or why is it suggested that three or four confederacies would be better than one? I am persuaded in my own mind that the people have always thought right on this subject, and that their universal and uniform attachment to the cause of the Union rests on great and weighty reasons, which I shall endeavor to develop and explain in some ensuing papers. They who promote the idea of substituting a number of distinct confederacies in the room of the plan of the convention seem clearly to foresee that the rejection of it would put the continuance of the Union in the utmost jeopardy. That certainly would be the case, and I sincerely wish that it may be as clearly foreseen by every good citizen that whenever the dissolution of the Union arrives, America will have reason to exclaim, in the words of the poet: "Farewell! A long farewell to all my greatness."

No. 3

The Same Subject Continued

The national security of the new nation, which Jay calls its "safety," will be best assured by a united country, which will protect citizens against external threats and internal uprisings of "direct and unlawful violence." The national government will be "more temperate and cool" than the states in settling disputes because "the pride of states, as well as of men, naturally disposes them to justify all their actions, and opposes their acknowledging, correcting, or repairing their errors and offenses. The national government, in such cases, will not be affected by this pride, but will proceed with moderation and candor to consider and decide on the means most proper to extricate them from the difficulties which threaten them."

Also, a national government will attract talent, "it will have the widest field for choice, and never experience that want of proper persons" common to the smaller, more isolated state governments.

It is not a new observation that the people of any country (if, like the Americans, intelligent and well-informed) seldom adopt and steadily persevere for many years in an erroneous opinion respecting their interests. That consideration naturally tends to create great respect for the high opinion which the people of America have so long and uniformly entertained of the importance of their continuing firmly united under one federal government, vested with sufficient powers for all general and national purposes.

The more attentively I consider and investigate the reasons which appear to have given birth to this opinion, the more I become convinced that they are cogent and conclusive.

National Security

Among the many objects to which a wise and free people find it necessary to direct their attention, that of providing for their *safety* seems to be the first. The *safety* of the people doubtless has relation to a great variety of circumstances and considerations, and consequently affords great latitude to those who wish to define it precisely and comprehensively.

At present I mean only to consider it as it respects security for the preservation of peace and tranquillity, as well as against dangers from *foreign arms and influence*, as from dangers of the *like kind* arising from domestic causes. As the former of these comes first in order, it is proper it should be the first discussed. Let us therefore proceed to examine whether the people are not right in their opinion that a cordial Union, under an efficient national government, affords them the best security that can be devised against *hostilities* from abroad.

The number of wars which have happened or will happen in the world will always be found to be in proportion to the number and weight of the causes, whether *real* or *pretended*, which *provoke* or *invite* them. If this remark be just, it becomes useful to inquire whether so many *just* causes of war are likely to be given by *united America* as by *disunited* America; for if it should turn out that united America will probably give the fewest, then it will follow that in this respect the Union tends most to preserve the people in a state of peace with other nations.

The *just* causes of war, for the most part, arise either from violations of treaties or from direct violence. America has already formed treaties with no less than six foreign nations, and all of them, except Prussia, are maritime, and therefore able to annoy and injure us. She has also extensive commerce with Portugal, Spain, and Britain, and, with respect to the two latter, has, in addition, the circumstance of neighborhood to attend to.

It is of high importance to the peace of America that she observe the laws of nations towards all these powers, and to me it appears evident that this will be more perfectly and punctually done by one national government than it could be either by thirteen separate States or by three or four distinct confederacies. For this opinion various reasons may be assigned.

National Government Will "Never Experience That Want of Proper Persons"

When once an efficient national government is established, the best men in the country will not only consent to serve, but also will generally be appointed to manage it; for, although town or country, or other contracted influence, may place men in State assemblies, or senates, or courts of justice, or executive departments, yet more general and extensive reputation for talents and other qualifications will be necessary to recommend men to offices under the national government—especially as it will have the widest field for choice, and never experience that want of proper persons which is not uncommon in some of the States. Hence, it will result that the administration, the political counsels, and the judicial decisions of the national government will be more wise, systematical, and judicious than those of individual States, and consequently more satisfactory with respect to other nations, as well as more *safe* with respect to us.

Under the national government, treaties and articles of treaties, as well as the laws of nations, will always be expounded in one sense and executed in the same manner—whereas adjudications on the same points and questions in thirteen States, or in three or four confederacies, will not always accord or be consistent; and that, as well from the variety of independent courts and judges appointed by different and independent governments as from the different local laws and interests which may affect and influence them. The wisdom of the convention in committing such questions to the jurisdiction and judgment of courts appointed by and responsible only to one national government cannot be too much commended.

The prospect of present loss or advantage may often tempt the governing party in one or two States to swerve from good faith and justice; but those temptations, not reaching the other States, and consequently having little or no influence on the national government, the temptation will be fruitless, and good faith and justice be preserved. The case of the treaty of peace with Britain adds great weight to this reasoning.

If even the governing party in a State should be disposed to resist such temptations, yet, as such temptations may, and commonly do, result from circumstances peculiar to the State, and may affect a great number of the inhabitants, the governing party may not always be able, if willing, to prevent the injustice meditated, or to punish the aggressors. But the national government, not being affected by those local circumstances, will neither be induced to commit the wrong themselves, nor want power or inclination to prevent or punish its commission by others.

So far, therefore, as either designed or accidental violations of treaties and of the laws of nations afford *just* causes of war, they are less to be apprehended under one general government than under several lesser ones, and in that respect the former most favors the *safety* of the people.

As to those just causes of war which proceed from direct and unlawful violence, it appears equally clear to me that one good national government affords vastly more security against dangers of that sort than can be derived from any other quarter.

Such violences are more frequently occasioned by the passions and interests of a part than of the whole, of one or two States than of the Union. Not a single Indian war has yet been produced by aggressions of the present federal government, feeble as it is; but there are several instances of Indian hostilities having been provoked by the improper conduct of individual States, who, either unable or unwilling to restrain or punish offenses, have given occasion to the slaughter of many innocent inhabitants.

The neighborhood of Spanish and British territories, bordering on some States and not on others, naturally confines the causes of quarrel more immediately to the borderers. The bordering States, if any, will be those who, under the impulse of sudden irritation, and a quick sense of apparent interest or injury, will be most likely, by direct violence, to excite war with those nations; and nothing can so effectually obviate that danger as a national government, whose wisdom and prudence will not be diminished by the passions which actuate the parties immediately interested.

But not only fewer just causes of war will be given by the national government, but it will also be more in their power to accommodate and settle them amicably. They will be more temperate and cool, and in that respect, as well as in others, will be more in capacity to act with circumspection than the offending State. The pride of states, as well as of men, naturally disposes them to justify all their actions, and opposes their acknowledging, correcting, or repairing their errors and offenses. The national government, in such cases, will not be affected by this pride, but will proceed with moderation and candor to consider and decide on the means most proper to extricate them from the difficulties which threaten them.

Besides, it is well known that acknowledgements, explanations, and compensations are often accepted as satisfactory from a strong united nation, which would be rejected as unsatisfactory if offered by a State or confederacy of little consideration or power. . . .

HAMILTON

No. 6

Concerning Dangers from War
Between the States

Hamilton lays out both his views on political society and his support of the commercial republic, arguing that "the spirit of commerce has a tendency to soften the manners of men, and to extinguish those inflammable humors which have so often kindled into wars. Commercial republics, like ours, will never be disposed to waste themselves in ruinous contentions with each other. They will be governed by mutual interest, and will cultivate a spirit of mutual amity and concord." This is one of The Federalist Papers' infrequent comments on the interplay of economics and politics. Possibly the authors believed the subject did not need much elaboration in these essays because most readers would agree that a stable, relatively prosperous economy was a prerequisite to a functioning republican government.

Hamilton signals the dangers of "domestic factions and convulsions," which Madison will consider in greater detail in Federalist No. 10. *Hamilton believes humans live, not in a utopian society, but are "ambitious, vindictive, and rapacious"; political stability does not come naturally to a people. He sends a dark warning, comparable to any of Madison's more developed reflections on the human condition: "To look for a continuation of harmony between a number of independent, unconnected sovereignties situated in the same neighborhood would be to disregard the uniform course of human events, and to set at defiance the accumulated experience of ages."*

The three last numbers of this paper have been dedicated to an enumeration of the dangers to which we should be exposed, in a state of disunion, from the arms and arts of foreign nations. I shall now proceed to delineate dangers of a different and, perhaps, still more alarming kind—those which will in all probability flow from dissensions between the States themselves and from domestic factions and convulsions. These have been already in some instances slightly anticipated; but they deserve a more particular and more full investigation.

"Ambitious, Vindictive, and Rapacious" Humanity

A man must be far gone in Utopian speculations who can seriously doubt that if these States should either be wholly disunited, or only united in partial confederacies, the subdivisions into which they might be thrown would have frequent and violent contests with each other. To presume a want of motives for such contests as an argument against their existence would be to forget that men are ambitious, vindictive, and rapacious. To look for a continuation of harmony between a number of independent, unconnected sovereignties situated in the same neighborhood would be to disregard the uniform course of human events, and to set at defiance the accumulated experience of ages.

The causes of hostility among nations are innumerable. There are some which have a general and almost constant operation upon the collective bodies of society. Of this description are the love of power or the desire of pre-eminence and dominion—the jealousy of power, or the desire of equality and safety. There are others which have a more circumscribed though an equally operative influence within their spheres. Such are the rivalships and competitions of commerce between commercial nations. And there are others, not less numerous than either of the former, which take their origin entirely in private passions; in the attachments, enmities, interests, hopes, and fears of leading individuals in the communities of which they are members. Men of this class, whether the favorites of a king or of a people, have in too many instances abused the confidence they possessed; and assuming the pretext of some public motive, have not scrupled to sacrifice the national tranquillity to personal advantage or personal gratification. . . .

The Commercial Republic

But notwithstanding the concurring testimony of experience, in this particular, there are still to be found visionary or designing men, who stand ready to advocate the paradox of perpetual peace between the States, though dismembered and alienated from each other. The genius of republics (say they) is pacific; the spirit of commerce has a tendency to soften the manners of men, and to extinguish those inflammable humors which have so often kindled into wars. Commercial republics, like ours, will never be disposed to waste themselves in ruinous contentions with each other. They will be governed by mutual interest, and will cultivate a spirit of mutual amity and concord.

Is it not (we may ask these projectors in politics) the true interest of all nations to cultivate the same benevolent and philosophic spirit? If this be their true interest, have they in fact pursued it? Has it not, on the contrary, invariably been found that momentary passions, and immediate interests, have a more active and imperious control over human conduct than general or remote considerations of policy, utility, or justice? Have republics in practice been less addicted to war than monarchies? Are not the former administered by *men* as well as the latter? Are there not aversions, predilections, rivalships, and desires of unjust acquisitions that affect nations as well as kings? Are not popular assemblies frequently subject to the impulses of rage, resentment, jealousy, avarice, and of other irregular and violent propensities? Is it not well known that their determinations are often governed by a few individuals in whom they place confidence, and are, of course, liable to be tinctured by the passions and views of those individuals? Has commerce hitherto done any thing more than change the objects of war? Is not the love of wealth as domineering and enterprising a passion as that of power or glory? Have there not been as many wars founded upon commercial motives since that has become the prevailing system of nations, as were before occasioned by the cupidity of territory or dominion? Has not the spirit of commerce, in many instances, administered new incentives to the appetite, both for the one and for the other? Let experience, the least fallible guide of human opinions, be appealed to for an answer to these inquiries.

Sparta, Athens, Rome, and Carthage were all republics; two of them, Athens and Carthage, of the commercial kind. Yet were they as often engaged in wars, offensive and defensive, as the neighboring monarchies of the same times. Sparta was little better than a well-regulated camp; and Rome was never sated of carnage and conquest.

Carthage, though a commercial republic, was the aggressor in the very war that ended in her destruction. Hannibal had carried her arms into the heart of Italy and to the gates of Rome, before Scipio, in turn, gave him an overthrow in the territories of Carthage and made a conquest of the commonwealth.

Venice, in later times, figured more than once in wars of ambition, till, becoming an object to the other Italian states, Pope Julius the Second found means to accomplish that formidable league,[1] which gave a deadly blow to the power and pride of this haughty republic.

The provinces of Holland, till they were overwhelmed in debts and taxes, took a leading and conspicuous part in the wars of Europe. They had furious contests with England for the dominion of the sea, and were among the most persevering and most implacable of the opponents of Louis XIV.

In the government of Britain the representatives of the people compose one branch of the national legislature. Commerce has been for ages the predominant pursuit of that country. Few nations, nevertheless, have been more frequently engaged in war; and the wars in which that kingdom has been engaged have, in numerous instances, proceeded from the people.

There have been, if I may so express it, almost as many popular as royal wars. The cries of the nation and the importunities of their representatives have, upon various occasions, dragged their monarchs into war, or continued them in it, contrary to their inclinations, and sometimes contrary to the real interests of the state. In that memorable struggle for superiority between the rival houses of *Austria* and *Bourbon,* which so long kept Europe in a flame, it is well known that the antipathies of the English against the French, seconding the ambition, or rather the avarice, of a favorite leader,[2] protracted the war beyond the limits marked out by sound policy, and for a considerable time in opposition to the views of the court.

The wars of these two last-mentioned nations have in a great measure grown out of commercial considerations—the desire of supplanting and the fear of being supplanted, either in particular branches of traffic or in the general advantages of trade and navigation, and sometimes even the more culpable desire of sharing in the commerce of other nations without their consent.

The last war but two between Britain and Spain sprang from the attempts of the English merchants to prosecute an illicit trade with the Spanish main. These unjustifiable practices on their part produced severity on the part of the Spaniards towards the subjects of Great Britain which were not more justifiable, because they exceeded the bounds of a just retaliation and were chargeable with inhumanity and cruelty. Many of the English who were taken on the Spanish coast were sent to dig in the mines of Potosi; and by the usual progress of a spirit of resentment, the innocent were, after a while, confounded with the guilty in indiscriminate punishment. The complaints of the merchants kindled a violent flame throughout the nation, which soon after broke out in the House of Commons, and was communicated from that body to the ministry. Letters of reprisal were granted, and a war ensued, which in its consequences overthrew all the alliances that but twenty years before had been formed, with sanguine expectations of the most beneficial fruits.

Neighboring States: Natural Enemies Unless Held Together in a Republic

From this summary of what has taken place in other countries, whose situations have borne the nearest resemblance to our own, what reason can we have to confide in those reveries which would seduce us into an expectation of peace and cordiality between the members of the present confederacy, in a state of separation? Have we not already seen enough of the fallacy and extravagance of those idle theories which have amused us with promises of an exemption from the imperfections, the weaknesses, and the evils incident to society in every shape? Is it not time to awake from the deceitful dream of a golden age and to adopt as a practical maxim for the direction of our political conduct that we, as well as the other inhabitants of the globe, are yet remote from the happy empire of perfect wisdom and perfect virtue?

Let the point of extreme depression to which our national dignity and credit have sunk, let the inconveniences felt everywhere from a lax and ill administration of government, let the revolt of a part of the State of North Carolina, the late menacing disturbances in Pennsylvania, and the actual insurrections and rebellions in Massachusetts, declare—!

So far is the general sense of mankind from corresponding with the tenets of those who endeavor to lull asleep our apprehensions of discord and hostility between the States, in the event of disunion, that it has from long observation of the progress of society become a sort of axiom in politics that vicinity, or nearness of situation, constitutes nations natural enemies. An intelligent writer expresses himself on this subject to this effect:

"Neighboring nations [says he] are naturally enemies of each other, unless their common weakness forces them to league in a confederate republic and their constitution prevents the differences that neighborhood occasions, extinguishing that secret jealousy which disposes all states to aggrandize themselves at the expense of their neighbors."[3] This passage, at the same time, points out the evil and suggests the remedy.

Small states, or states of less natural strength, under vigorous governments, and with the assistance of disciplined armies, have often triumphed over large states, or states of greater natural strength, which have been destitute of these advantages. Neither the pride nor the safety of the more important States, or confederacies, would permit them long to submit to this mortifying and adventitious superiority. They would quickly resort to means similar to those by which it had been effected, to reinstate themselves in their lost pre-eminence. Thus we should, in a little time, see established in every part of this country the same engines of despotism which have been the scourge of the old world. This, at least, would be the natural course of things; and our reasonings will be the more likely to be just in proportion as they are accommodated to this standard.

These are not vague inferences drawn from supposed or speculative defects in a Constitution, the whole power of which is lodged in the hands of a people, or their representatives and delegates, but they are solid conclusions drawn from the natural and necessary progress of human affairs.

It may, perhaps, be asked, by way of objection to this, why did not standing armies spring up out of the contentions which so often distracted the ancient republics of Greece? Different answers, equally satisfactory, may be given to this question. The industrious habits of the people of the present day, absorbed in the pursuits of gain and devoted to the improvements of agriculture and commerce, are incompatible with the condition of a nation of soldiers, which was the true condition of the people of those republics. The means of revenue, which have been so greatly multiplied by the increase of gold and silver and of the arts of industry, and the science of finance, which is the offspring of modern times, concurring with the habits of nations, have produced an entire revolution in the system of war, and have rendered disciplined armies, distinct from the body of the citizens, the inseparable companion of frequent hostility.

Armies in Stable and Unstable Countries

There is a wide difference, also, between military establishments in a country seldom exposed by its situation to internal invasions, and in one which is often subject to them and always apprehensive of them. The rulers of the former can have no good pretext, if they are even so inclined, to keep on foot armies so numerous as must of necessity be maintained in the latter. These armies being, in the first case, rarely if at all called into activity for interior defense, the people are in no danger of being broken to military

No. 8

The Effects of Internal War in Producing Standing Armies and Other Institutions Unfriendly to Liberty

Hamilton makes the case for standing armies "and the correspondent appendages of military establishments." He states, "Safety from external danger is the most powerful director of national conduct." A standing army will discourage surprise invasions and suppress mobs and insurrections; without such a force "we should, in a little time, see established in every part of this country the same engines of despotism which have been the scourge of the old world." Hamilton favors a small army under civilian control. He tells readers, with the memory of a recent devastating war fresh in mind, "The laws are not accustomed to relaxation in favor of military exigencies; the civil state remains in full vigor." Warfare is to be avoided if possible; in Europe, "war . . . is no longer a history of nations subdued and empires overtaken, but of towns taken and retaken, of battles that decide nothing, of retreats more beneficial than victories, of much effort and little acquisition." In America war "would be desultory and predatory. Plunder and devastation ever march in the train of irregulars. The calamities of individuals would make the principal figure in the events which would characterize our military exploits."

Hamilton believes a commercially active, prosperous people will show little interest in war, because such people, "absorbed in the pursuits of gain

and devoted to the improvements of agriculture and commerce, are incompatible with the condition of a nation of soldiers." He cautions, "It is in the nature of war to increase the executive at the expense of the legislative authority," which can lead toward authoritarian governments. He warns against the dangers of an overly strong military, especially because civil rights would be degraded and a military state created.

Assuming therefore as an established truth that the several States, in case of disunion, or such combinations of them as might happen to be formed out of the wreck of the general Confederacy, would be subject to those vicissitudes of peace and war, of friendship and enmity with each other, which have fallen to the lot of all neighboring nations not united under one government, let us enter into a concise detail of some of the consequences that would attend such a situation.

The Need for Standing Armies

War between the States, in the first period of their separate existence, would be accompanied with much greater distresses than it commonly is in those countries where regular military establishments have long obtained. The disciplined armies always kept on foot on the continent of Europe, though they bear a malignant aspect to liberty and economy, have, notwithstanding, been productive of the signal advantage of rendering sudden conquests impracticable, and of preventing that rapid desolation which used to mark the progress of war prior to their introduction. The art of fortification has contributed to the same ends. The nations of Europe are encircled with chains of fortified places, which mutually obstruct invasion. Campaigns are wasted in reducing two or three frontier garrisons to gain admittance into an enemy's country. Similar impediments occur at every step to exhaust the strength and delay the progress of an invader. Formerly an invading army would penetrate into the heart of a neighboring country almost as soon as intelligence of its approach could be received; but now a comparatively small force of disciplined troops, acting on the defensive, with the aid of posts, is able to impede, and finally to frustrate, the enterprises of one much more considerable. The history of war in that quarter of the globe is no longer a history of nations subdued and empires overturned, but of towns taken and retaken, of battles that decide nothing, of retreats more beneficial than victories, of much effort and little acquisition.

In this country the scene would be altogether reversed. The jealou military establishments would postpone them as long as possible. The of fortifications, leaving the frontiers of one State open to another, w facilitate inroads. The populous States would, with little difficulty, over their less populous neighbors. Conquests would be as easy to be mad difficult to be retained. War, therefore, would be desultory and predate Plunder and devastation ever march in the train of irregulars. The cala ties of individuals would make the principal figure in the events wh would characterize our military exploits.

This picture is not too highly wrought; though, I confess, it would n long remain a just one. Safety from external danger is the most powerfu director of national conduct. Even the ardent love of liberty will, after time, give way to its dictates. The violent destruction of life and property incident to war, the continual effort and alarm attendant on a state o continual danger, will compel nations the most attached to liberty to resort for repose and security to institutions which have a tendency to destroy their civil and political rights. To be more safe, they at length become willing to run the risk of being less free.

Standing Armies

The institutions chiefly alluded to are standing armies and the correspondent appendages of military establishments. Standing armies, it is said, are not provided against in the new Constitution; and it is thence inferred that they may exist under it. This inference, from the very form of the proposition, is, at best, problematical and uncertain.[1] But standing armies, it may be replied, must inevitably result from a dissolution of the Confederacy. Frequent war and constant apprehension, which require a state of as constant preparation, will infallibly produce them. The weaker States, or confederacies, would first have recourse to them to put themselves upon an equality with their more potent neighbors. They would endeavor to supply the inferiority of population and resources by a more regular and effective system of defense, by disciplined troops, and by fortifications. They would, at the same time, be necessitated to strengthen the executive arm of government, in doing which their constitutions would acquire a progressive direction towards monarchy. It is of the nature of war to increase the executive at the expense of the legislative authority.

The expedients which have been mentioned would soon give the States, or confederacies, that made use of them a superiority over their neighbors.

subordination. The laws are not accustomed to relaxation in favor of military exigencies; the civil state remains in full vigor, neither corrupted, nor confounded with the principles or propensities of the other state. The smallness of the army renders the natural strength of the community an overmatch for it; and the citizens, not habituated to look up to the military power for protection, or to submit to its oppressions, neither love nor fear the soldiery; they view them with a spirit of jealous acquiescence in a necessary evil and stand ready to resist a power which they suppose may be exerted to the prejudice of their rights.

The army under such circumstances may usefully aid the magistrate to suppress a small faction, or an occasional mob, or insurrection; but it will be unable to enforce encroachments against the united efforts of the great body of the people.

In a country in the predicament last described, the contrary of all this happens. The perpetual menacings of danger oblige the government to be always prepared to repel it; its armies must be numerous enough for instant defense. The continual necessity for their services enhances the importance of the soldier, and proportionably degrades the condition of the citizen. The military state becomes elevated above the civil. The inhabitants of territories, often the theater of war, are unavoidably subjected to frequent infringements of their rights, which serve to weaken their sense of those rights; and by degrees the people are brought to consider the soldiery not only as their protectors but as their superiors. The transition from this disposition to that of considering them masters is neither remote nor difficult; but it is very difficult to prevail upon a people under such impressions to make a bold or effectual resistance to usurpations supported by the military power.

The kingdom of Great Britain falls within the first description. An insular situation, and a powerful marine, guarding it in a great measure against the possibility of foreign invasion, supersede the necessity of a numerous army within the kingdom. A sufficient force to make head against a sudden descent, till the militia could have time to rally and embody, is all that has been deemed requisite. No motive of national policy has demanded, nor would public opinion have tolerated, a larger number of troops upon its domestic establishment. There has been, for a long time past, little room for the operation of the other causes, which have been enumerated as the consequences of internal war. This peculiar felicity of situation has, in a great degree, contributed to preserve the liberty which that country to this day enjoys, in spite of the prevalent venality and corruption. If, on the contrary, Britain had been situated on the continent, and had been compelled, as she would have been, by that situation, to make her military establishments at home coextensive with those of the other great powers of Europe, she, like them, would in all probability be, at this day, a victim to the absolute power of a single man. 'Tis possible, though not easy, that the people of that island may be enslaved from other causes; but it cannot be by the prowess of an army so inconsiderable as that which has been usually kept up within the kingdom.

"If We Are Wise Enough to Preserve the Union"

If we are wise enough to preserve the Union we may for ages enjoy an advantage similar to that of an insulated situation. Europe is at a great distance from us. Her colonies in our vicinity will be likely to continue too much disproportioned in strength to be able to give us any dangerous annoyance. Extensive military establishments cannot, in this position, be necessary to our security. But if we should be disunited, and the integral parts should either remain separated, or, which is most probable, should be thrown together into two or three confederacies, we should be, in a short course of time, in the predicament of the continental powers of Europe— our liberties would be a prey to the means of defending ourselves against the ambition and jealousy of each other.

This is an idea not superficial nor futile, but solid and weighty. It deserves the most serious and mature consideration of every prudent and honest man of whatever party. If such men will make a firm and solemn pause, and meditate dispassionately on the importance of this interesting idea; if they will contemplate it in all its attitudes, and trace it to all its consequences, they will not hesitate to part with trivial objections to a Constitution, the rejection of which would in all probability put a final period to the Union. The airy phantoms that flit before the distempered imaginations of some of its adversaries would quickly give place to the more substantial prospects of dangers, real, certain, and formidable.

No. 9

The Utility of the Union as a Safeguard Against Domestic Faction and Insurrection

An attraction of the new union is its size, which means "the enlargement of the orbit within which . . . systems [of civil government] are to revolve." However, Hamilton believes even a large, stable government can only have popular support if political powers are separated through "the regular distribution of power into distinct departments." Additionally, there must be "legislative balances and checks." These are the "means, and powerful means, by which the excellencies of republican government may be retained and its imperfections lessened or avoided." Additional separation of powers includes courts "composed of judges holding their offices during good behavior," which means for long terms, and a legislature elected by the people. Hamilton cites Montesquieu's concept of a confederate republic, which represents "a luminous abridgment of the principal arguments in favor of the Union," in which several small states unite for the advantage of size and strength, while retaining their basic independence. "This fully corresponds, in every rational import of the terms, with the idea of a federal government."

A firm Union will be of the utmost moment to the peace and liberty of the States as a barrier against domestic faction and insurrection. It is impossible to read the history of the petty republics of Greece and Italy without feeling sensations of horror and disgust at the distractions with which they were continually agitated, and at the rapid succession of revolutions by which they were kept in a state of perpetual vibration between the extremes of tyranny and anarchy. If they exhibit occasional calms, these only serve as short-lived contrasts to the furious storms that are to succeed. If now and then intervals of felicity open themselves to view, we behold them with a mixture of regret, arising from the reflection that the pleasing scenes before us are soon to be overwhelmed by the tempestuous waves of sedition and party rage. If momentary rays of glory break forth from the gloom, while they dazzle us with a transient and fleeting brilliancy, they at the same time admonish us to lament that the vices of government should pervert the direction and tarnish the luster of those bright talents and exalted endowments for which the favored soils that produced them have been so justly celebrated.

Despotism Versus Liberty

From the disorders that disfigure the annals of those republics the advocates of despotism have drawn arguments, not only against the forms of republican government, but against the very principles of civil liberty. They have decried all free government as inconsistent with the order of society, and have indulged themselves in malicious exultation over its friends and partisans. Happily for mankind, stupendous fabrics reared on the basis of liberty, which have flourished for ages, have, in a few glorious instances, refuted their gloomy sophisms. And, I trust, America will be the broad and solid foundation of other edifices, not less magnificent, which will be equally permanent monuments of their errors.

But it is not to be denied that the portraits they have sketched of republican government were too just copies of the originals from which they were taken. If it had been found impracticable to have devised models of a more perfect structure, the enlightened friends to liberty would have been obliged to abandon the cause of that species of government as indefensible. The science of politics, however, like most other sciences, has received great improvement. The efficacy of various principles is now well understood, which were either not known at all, or imperfectly known to the ancients. The regular distribution of power into distinct departments; the introduction of legislative balances and checks; the institution of courts composed of judges holding their offices during good behavior; the